When Women
Ruled the Pacific

When Women Ruled the Pacific

*Power and Politics
in Nineteenth-Century
Tahiti and Hawai'i*

JOY SCHULZ

University of Nebraska Press
LINCOLN

The University of Nebraska Press is part of a land-grant institution with campuses and programs on the past, present, and future homelands of the Pawnee, Ponca, Otoe-Missouria, Omaha, Dakota, Lakota, Kaw, Cheyenne, and Arapaho Peoples, as well as those of the relocated Ho-Chunk, Sac and Fox, and Iowa Peoples.

♾

Library of Congress Cataloging-in-Publication Data
Names: Schulz, Joy, author.
Title: When women ruled the Pacific: power and politics in nineteenth-century Tahiti and Hawai'i / Joy Schulz.
Description: Lincoln: University of Nebraska Press, [2023] | Series: Studies in Pacific worlds | Includes bibliographical references and index.
Identifiers: LCCN 2022048792
ISBN 9781496231802 (hardback)
ISBN 9781496236708 (epub)
ISBN 9781496236715 (pdf)
Subjects: LCSH: Queens—Tahiti (French Polynesia: Island)—Biography. | Queens—Hawaii—Biography. | Tahiti (French Polynesia: Island)—Kings and rulers—Biography. | Hawaii—Kings and rulers—Biography. | Tahiti (French Polynesia: Island)—Politics and government. | Hawaii—Politics and government—To 1893. | BISAC: HISTORY / United States / State & Local / West (AK, CA, CO, HI, ID, MT, NV, UT, WY) | SOCIAL SCIENCE / Women's Studies
Classification: LCC DU870 .S374 2023 | DDC 996.20099—dc23/eng/20230321
LC record available at https://lccn.loc.gov/2022048792

Set in Adobe Caslon by A. Shahan.

To my daughters, Sophia and Penelope

Oh, honest Americans, as Christians hear me for my down-trodden people! Their form of government is as dear to them as yours is precious to you. Quite as warmly as you love your country, so they love theirs. . . .

The people to whom your fathers told of the living God, and taught to call "Father," and whom the sons now seek to despoil and destroy, are crying aloud to Him in their time of trouble; and He will keep His promise, and will listen to the voices of His Hawaiian children lamenting for their homes.

It is for them that I would give the last drop of my blood; it is for them that I would spend, nay, am spending, everything belonging to me. Will it be in vain? It is for the American people and their representatives in Congress to answer these questions. As they deal with me and my people, kindly, gener-ously, and justly, so may the Great Ruler of all nations deal with the grand and glorious nation of the United States of America.

—QUEEN LILIʻUOKALANI (1898)

Contents

Illustrations

Acknowledgments

Many people have made this book possible. I would like to thank my editor, Bridget Barry, who, for the second time, believed in me. I also would like to thank Jane Curran, Sara Springsteen, Annie Shahan, Tish Fobben, and the rest of the staff at the University of Nebraska Press for their encouragement and aid in publication. I offer a special word of gratitude to the anonymous readers on this project who took the time to provide their constructive feedback. Thank you to Jane Franklin, Tom McDonnell, Randy Schmailzl, and the Metropolitan Community College Board of Governors for granting me the time to complete this project. Thank you, also, to Tim Borstelmann, Margaret Jacobs, and James Le Sueur, my mentors.

For friendship and inspiration within the field, I would like to thank Anne Foster, Jennifer Thigpen, and Emily Manktelow. And to Rick Antonson, I also say thank you for encouraging me to pursue this project.

Above all, I thank my husband, Marc, for his unwavering support, and I thank my parents and family for their generosity of love and time.

When Women
Ruled the Pacific

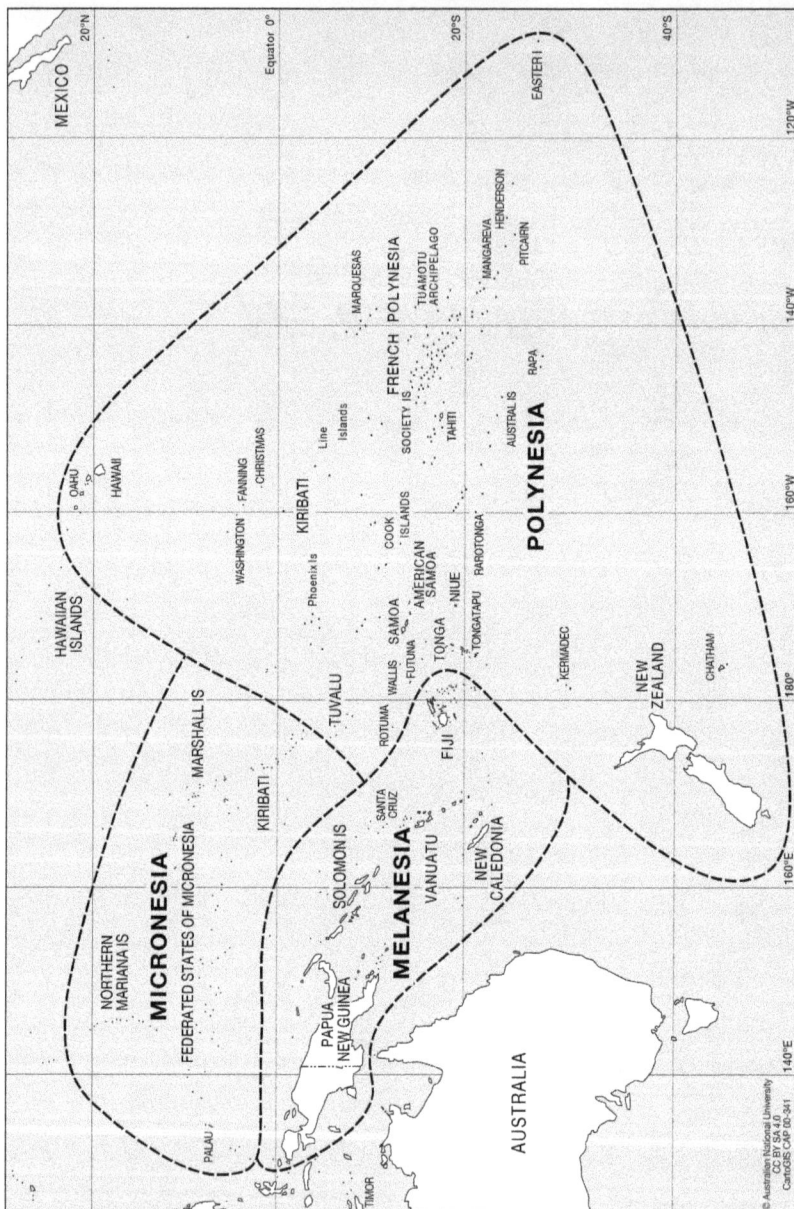

1. Pacific worlds. Map reproduced with the permission of CartoGIS
Services, Scholarly Information Services, The Australian National
University, http://asiapacific.anu.edu.au/mapsonline/.

Introduction

Woman in Red

Na to tamahine ka pai i ta kina mai ai teni ke keno ki konei.
[It was this lovely girl who brought the seal here.]
—MAORI PROVERB

In 1767 Captain Samuel Wallis left England with secret orders from King George III to sail the HMS *Dolphin* into the southern Pacific Ocean and search for a mythical seventh continent. Instead Wallis encountered Tahiti. Two years later James Cook, aboard the HMS *Endeavor*, stopped in Tahiti before pushing onward to complete the king's command when he sighted Australia. Upon anchoring in Matavai Bay, Tahiti, both captains met a stunning woman dressed in red tapa (cloth). She was Tahiti's high chief, Tevahine-'ai-roro-atua-i-Ahurai, also known as Purea (c. 1720–c. 1775).[1]

Purea's decision to aid the English set in motion a century of change for England and Tahiti as each nation became aware of the other for the first time. After Captain Cook became the first white person to visit the Hawaiian Islands in 1778, the United States, too, began to seek influence among Polynesian peoples. Soon English Protestant missionaries arrived in Tahiti, and American Protestant missionaries established a mission in the Hawaiian Islands. The American missionaries were given permission to land in the islands by another imposing woman, Ka'ahumanu (1768–1832), the *kuhina nui* (premier) of the Hawaiian kingdom.[2]

In these Pacific archipelagoes, British imperialists visualized a new context for colonialism. While Cook's exploration of Australia provided the British government with land for its convicts and debtors (the refuse of England, as lawmakers saw them) and a new colonial continent to fill the void left by England's loss of the newly independent United States, the smaller Polynesian islands could be utilized to supply English seamen and settlers on their voyages across the British Empire, which now circled the globe. During the nineteenth century Indigenous populations experienced the impact of these British efforts, as well as similar imperial projects undertaken by the United States and France.[3]

Foreign contact had catastrophic effects on Polynesian peoples and cultures. In Tahiti and Hawai'i women rulers attempted to mitigate the effects of these encounters. Purea, for example, was the only Tahitian high chief willing to meet with Samuel Wallis and his crew. In the Hawaiian Islands American missionaries at first failed to understand that Ka'ahumanu was the gatekeeper for access to her ward, King Kamehameha II. Both Purea and Ka'ahumanu maintained their political authority amid the confusing and destabilizing influence of English and American visitors and were able to preserve their *mana* (spiritual authority) while negotiating with foreigners.[4]

Unfortunately, this precarious balance of power did not last long. As the century progressed, foreign diseases devastated the Tahitian and Hawaiian populations, and the aims of powerful European fleets jockeyed for more formal control over Polynesian way stations. Yet, amazingly, the last independent, Indigenous rulers of Tahiti and Hawai'i were both women. After years of fighting against French influence, Vahine-o-Punuatera'itua 'Aimata (1813–77), known as 'Aimata, or Pōmare IV, ceded her twenty-year rule of Tahiti to France in 1847. In a bloodless revolution, Queen Lili'uokalani, born Lili'u Loloku Walania Kamaka'eha (1838–1917), relinquished her Hawaiian throne to the United States in 1893, after white residents resisted her efforts to strengthen the monarchy and increase Indigenous political power.[5]

Women rulers in sites of European and American colonial expansion serve as counterweights to our understanding of nineteenth-century gender roles in Europe and America. While women in power were not unheard of in Europe—Queen Victoria sat on the English throne for much of the nineteenth century—Polynesian women based their rule not only upon birth and succession, but also consent and *mana*. Like their European counterparts, Polynesian rulers fought arguments of lineage, as well as battles for territorial control, yet the freedom of Polynesian women in general and as rulers in particular was unlike anything Europeans and Americans had seen. Consequently, white chroniclers of contact had difficulty explaining their encounters, initially praising yet ultimately condemning Polynesian gender systems.[6]

Complicating the European and American understanding of Polynesian cultural practices was the role of religion. While sailors praised the absence of Christian moral values in Polynesia, the larger English and American populations viewed the islands as mission fields destined for spiritual destruction without the evangelizing and civilizing ministries of newly formed missionary organizations, such as the London Missionary Society (LMS), created by English Anglicans and Methodists in 1795, and the American Board of Commissioners for Foreign Missions (ABCFM), founded by U.S. Congregationalists and Presbyterians in 1810.[7]

Despite the eventual acceptance of Christianity by Tahitian and Hawaiian chiefs, Euro-American concerns regarding Polynesian independence and the authority of Polynesian women continued. In the end France and the United States rejected Tahitian and Hawaiian arguments that they were equal members of the same spiritual family as their white missionary allies and that their queens deserved the same diplomatic respect as the monarchs of Europe. Instead France and the United States ended Tahitian and Hawaiian sovereignty, as well as the constitutional role of their queens.[8]

Transcolonial Queenship and the Imperial Past

The historiography regarding the English and French colonization of Tahiti largely reflects the logs and memoirs of white naval captains, sailors, and missionaries. Early narratives, such as those by Colin Newbury, Douglas Oliver, Niel Gunson, and, more recently, Anne Salmond, are written primarily through the eyes of those men, although the authors are sensitive to Polynesian political structures and cultural nuances.[9]

In recent years key texts developing the political motivations of early Hawaiian rulers have added important corrections to earlier histories of American contact with the Hawaiian Islands that were written predominantly from the perspectives of white men. Jennifer Thigpen and Neolani Arista, particularly, add gendered perspectives to earlier literature on naval and missionary encounters.[10]

Nevertheless, no previous studies have shown the dominance of Polynesian women in wielding political power during these encounters and despite the unique threat foreigners posed to their rule and their people's independence. The following chapters attempt to correct the narrative by highlighting a historically unparalleled *transcolonial queenship* that existed among these women. By rewriting traditional histories of contact from the women's perspectives, I hope to demonstrate that patriarchal power was not normative in precontact Polynesia.

This book is most obviously about transnational encounters in the Pacific that altered Indigenous political and gender norms at sites of contact during the eighteenth and nineteenth centuries. It is also about religion. When conflict between the eternal bonds of a heavenly kingdom came into conflict with earthly opportunities for material gain, Polynesian rulers fought against their territorial losses by appealing to a shared Christian faith. British, French, and American imperialists argued against Polynesian independence by pointing to violations of Christian constructs of gender. Ultimately Christian betrayed Christian, as Queen Victoria and the British Foreign Office and President William McKinley and the U.S. Senate refused to support their weaker island allies.[11]

The four Polynesian chiefs described in the following pages held enormous domestic and foreign power at a time when industrializing nations were grappling for ports, plantations, and peoples to whom they could sell their manufactured goods. These Polynesian "queens"[12] navigated the tumultuous waters of international relations when the practice of international relations was still quite new to European and American statesmen. The women governed their people amid shifting loyalties, outright betrayals, and the ascendancy of imperial racism. These rulers deserve their rightful place in the world's pantheon of political leaders and, distinctively, as women who ruled the Pacific.

Islands

Polynesian cultures existed in isolation from the rest of the world but developed in tangent to each other in the millennium prior to European contact. The ancient art of Polynesian navigation can best be summarized as *brilliant*. As Polynesian peoples spread across the Pacific via their extensive knowledge of the stars and in their own handmade canoes, they accomplished what Europeans could not for hundreds of years.[13]

The Society Islands prior to European contact were divided among kinship groups between the Leeward Islands, containing Huahine, Taha'a, Ra'itaia, and Bora Bora, and the Winward Islands, comprising Tahiti and Mo'orea. Tahiti itself was further divided into six major kinship networks and between twenty to thirty districts. Religion dominated the political culture of precontact Tahiti.[14]

The Tahitian people descended from the father god Ta'aroa, who created their homeland, Havai'i, and formed Ti'i, the first man. Ti'i slept with the moon goddess, Hina, and their descendants were the first Tahitians to wear the red and yellow feather girdles that signified the highest chiefly status. Thus, genealogies were of the upmost importance to determining one's rank before the gods and in society. Later the Tamatoa clan from Ra'itaia brought to Tahiti the cult of Oro, which included a call to seek unification under one chief. Because Oro was the god of war, unification by force, and not just lineage, contained spiritual *mana* for Oro worshippers. By the time of European arrival, chiefly lineages linked to the Tamatoa clan were of the highest status in Tahiti, and one high-ranking chief, Purea, was poised to succeed in her goal of Tahitian unification.[15]

The Hawaiian Islands were not unified when Captain Cook arrived, and the main islands also were subdivided into districts. Wākea, the sky father, and Papa, the earth mother, created the Hawaiian Islands. Like Tahiti, genealogies stemming from the children of Wākea and his daughter, Ho'ohōkūkalani, determined one's rank in society. Strict taboos in both Tahitian and Hawaiian societies segregated the chiefly classes from commoners, as well as men from women. Lilikalā Kame'eleihiwa writes that Tahitians may have introduced these gender taboos to the Hawaiian people around the year 1200.[16]

The *kapu* (taboos) in Hawai'i and *tapu* (taboos) in Tahiti point to linkages of culture, religion, and language among Polynesian peoples, and these rich connections were made long before the first Europeans arrived. Hawaiian oral traditions, for example, describe the arrival of the volcano goddess, Pele, from Bora Bora. The Hawaiian term *kahiki* ("Tahiti") referred to a southern land from where their Hawaiian gods originated. Captain Cook, the first European captain to visit both the Society and Hawaiian Islands, noticed these similarities. "How can we account for this Nation spreading itself so far over this vast ocean?" he marveled.[17]

Matriarchal power was another important aspect of Polynesian culture that operated in both archipelagos at the point of European contact. A mother's lineage was as important as a father's genealogy in determining chiefly status. In fact, in studying leading Polynesian family groups, Niel Gunson argues that rank was inherited through one's mother, making the status of chiefly women "equal if not superior to that of chiefly men." Kamehameha I would be the first Hawaiian chief to unite the Hawaiian

Islands using military conquest. Kamehameha took at least twenty wives in strategic alliances, but he appointed as his heir the son from his wife, Keōpūolani, who possessed the highest chiefly status in the islands.[18]

Tahitians and Hawaiians held women in high regard. Women were believed to possess the *mana* necessary to balance men just as the gods balanced each other. Chiefly women could hold governing authority and were known as powerful warriors. Nevertheless, in both the Society and Hawaiian Islands, women were prohibited from conducting or attending religious rituals. These restrictions ultimately limited the political power of women, as religion was intricately related to the possession and distribution of lands, reception of gifts, and eating privileges associated with men.[19]

Missionaries

English and American efforts to spread Christianity to peoples on Pacific Ocean islands formally materialized after the Second Great Awakening, which spread from England to the United States during the first decade of the nineteenth century. Birthed from a transoceanic movement that emphasized demonstrable conversion, moral perfectibility, and missionary sacrifice, Christian converts in the early nineteenth century pledged their lives to foreign lands and peoples. As explorers brought back tales of exotic, unchristian cultures, Protestant churches in both nations formed organizations and raised contributions to send missionaries to those places. Tahiti was the first destination for missionaries from the London Missionary Society, while Indian nations in the American West were the earliest points of contact for missionaries from the American Board of Commissioners for Foreign Missions, followed by the Hawaiian Islands. Both societies raised tremendous amounts of interest and support from their citizens and governments. Both organizations remained in close contact with each other throughout this early missionary period.[20]

The first missionaries to the Society and Hawaiian Islands arrived with undeniable sincerity. They sold their personal belongings, paid off debts, and embarked on lengthy voyages to islands they planned to live on for the rest of their lives. The missionaries' stated intentions were to raise their children as islanders, convert the native populations to Christianity, and avoid entanglements with Indigenous governments. In their first and last goals, the missionaries failed miserably, but their long-term efforts to spread Christianity in the Pacific proved successful. As Gunson writes, Protestant missionary activity in the Pacific was "revolutionary in its effect upon the culture and transformation of the island peoples." Today the populations of French Polynesia and Hawai'i are majority Christian.[21]

On the other hand, missionary endeavors came with long-term political implications. Andrew Porter calls the British and American missionary efforts to remain nonpolitical in their new surroundings "naive."[22] Perhaps *discarded* is a better way to describe the increasingly complicated relationships missionaries formed with Tahitian and Hawaiian rulers, particularly the ones discussed in the following pages. The legacy of missionary involvement in Tahiti and Hawai'i cannot be overstated.

International Context

Ferdinand Magellan was the first European to sail around the world, departing from Spain in 1519. It took the Portuguese explorer and his crew three years to accomplish the feat, and Magellan died along the way. By the early nineteenth century, new events made circumnavigation more desirable: namely, trade with China for goods acquired in the Pacific region. Sandalwood from the Hawaiian Islands, sea cucumbers from Fiji, and otter pelts from the Pacific Northwest became valuable commodities in East Asia, as well as in the United States and Europe. The whaling industry followed.[23]

Early British explorations were largely scientific in nature, but after the American War for Independence concluded in 1783, global trade networks became new sites of conflict between the former British colonists and competing English merchants. While Tahiti and Hawai'i both fell early under the protection of the British government, Hawai'i's proximity to North America, especially after the United States annexed California in 1848, meant that England's best opportunity for continued influence in the Hawaiian Islands lay in securing an agreement from the United States to maintain the Hawaiian kingdom's independence. Various claims to land ownership also continued in the Pacific Northwest among Spain, England, Russia, and the United States during the first half of the nineteenth century.[24]

France entered late into the race for Pacific Ocean trade agreements and ports. By the time France recovered from the French Revolution and Napoleonic wars, American and British missionaries already had fanned out across the Pacific. Consequently, France's colonial claims largely lay in securing equal rights for Roman Catholics and negotiating treaties that gave France the same trade status as other colonial powers.[25]

Despite the interest of U.S. and European powers in extending commercial trade routes around the world, the impracticality of possessing and maintaining Pacific colonies persisted. England focused on Australia and New Zealand, while the United States, until 1898, and with the exception of Alaska, restricted its ambitions to contiguous North America. France and Germany, meanwhile, became more aggressive as the century progressed.[26]

Ultimately it was the merchants, missionaries, and naval captains who propelled individual European nations and the U.S. government toward more formal involvement in the Pacific. Their grandiose plans and gestures often exceeded or directly violated the foreign policy directives of their respective states. Many historians have tackled this idea of "informal empire" and the impact periphery populations can have upon the metropole.[27]

The paradox of this imperial push into the Pacific is that trade with China never materialized into the long-term economic returns for which European and American merchants had hoped. Extractors found sandalwood, otters, and whales more difficult to capture as their populations exponentially decreased, and China retained a firm grip on its bullion. Pacific ports, however, remained critical to major powers in an increasingly globalized, nineteenth-century world. Pacific peoples responded to the whims of Europeans and Americans as a result.[28]

Patriarchal Imperialism

Although not as multifaceted as contemporary debates, gender during the nineteenth century was no less contested in Anglo-European societies. In the United States, early nineteenth-century industrialization led to new roles within American families and new arguments about their supposed implications for gender. For American women this meant a renewed emphasis on the domestic sphere, particularly child rearing, as husbands became the primary wage earners. With the availability of farmland diminishing within existing states, American men took jobs in urban factories. The physical divide between home and paid labor became a gender divide, "separate spheres of influence" that would become the dominant gender narrative in the United States for at least one hundred years. American missionaries inserted these gender roles into their message and practice.[29]

The ideal of domesticity contained commercial elements as well. And much of the romanticized efforts of parents to provide a model domestic space for their children extended from the influence of French philosopher

Jean-Jacques Rousseau, whose earlier works on childhood, in the words of Julie Hardwick, "articulated a new model of family life as the basis for a new kind of politics that quickly became wildly popular in England as well as France." Nineteenth-century magazines capitalized on advertising revenue by publishing visions of domestic bliss that included colonial imports. Consequently, global commerce became a middle-class political paradigm. After the American Revolution, American merchants wanted access to such trade as well.[30]

In Britain, the nineteenth century was one of colonial expansion. In public discourse English men continued to elevate English women in terms of their race and moral virtue and took those ideals to colonial frontiers where they wrote concepts of racial superiority into marriage and family law. English missionaries taught native children that moral uplift could be achieved through domestic service for girls and agricultural or manual labor for boys.[31]

Victoria's ascendency to the British throne in 1837 had little impact on English views of gender. While the women's movement, for a time, used Victoria as an example of progress, it ultimately realized that the British Crown was severely limited under a constitutional monarchy and that Victoria herself was not a friend of the movement or a supporter of its aims.[32]

By the mid-nineteenth century, gender debates in the United States again shifted. Masculine fears that urban life created effeminacy influenced monumental historic movements, such as westward expansion and the Spanish-American War. In those imagined spaces that became literal battlefields, manhood again was redefined as American men asserted themselves against Indian, Chinese, and Filipino families.[33]

Westward expansion also created economic and political opportunities for American women. The 1862 Homestead Act opened lands for single and widowed women, and new territories began granting women suffrage. U.S. women's colleges, too, evolved, arguing that a full education was important for women if they were to properly raise their families or teach others how to do so. In Victorian England, Englishwomen used the low condition of Britain's colonial women as a platform from which to discuss feminist issues. And in the American West, American women offered a uniquely "female moral authority" when taking their middle-class views of civilization to Indian and immigrant populations.[34]

Such morality came with a high price for Indigenous cultures, as English and American missionaries were successful, to vast degrees, in removing native children from their parents and educating them according to their own Anglo-European views of race. In places as far flung as the Great Plains, Australia, and the Philippines, white missionaries incorporated into their proselytizing efforts the view that children of color should be trained for manual, not intellectual, labor.[35]

Matriarchal Resistance

Of course, Polynesian cultures maintained their own gender systems prior to Anglo-European arrival. In domestic spheres Polynesian husbands and wives lived largely segregated lifestyles, due to religious restrictions on cooking and eating. As a result, Polynesian men often had additional domestic duties. Conversely Polynesian women held prominent political positions.[36]

Both Tahitian and Hawaiian cultures allowed for more than binary gender divisions. Men in both societies could choose to occupy positions that allowed them domestic contact with women and sexual relations with men. In Tahiti the *mahu* were men who resided with men but took on women's roles in their relations with them. In the Hawaiian Islands, the word *aikāne* meant male friendship but could also signify a sexual act between two men. Sodomy and homosexual relations among both Tahitian and Hawaiian chiefly classes were common. Tahitian chief Pōmare II and Hawaiian king Kamehameha III both had male lovers.[37]

Polynesian men also could pursue occupations associated with women. Native historian Samuel Kamakau describes the "dyers and printers of Ehu" who were men disinclined to follow traditional masculine pursuits, such as deep-sea fishing and taro planting. Instead the men became experts in clothing design, an occupation predominantly populated by women.[38]

When Anglo-European and Polynesian gender systems collided at transnational contact, the aftermath was complicated both for missionary and Indigenous populations. Newer trends in scholarship address these multifaceted responses. As Emily Manktelow observes, the "politics of identity at play" were "complex, fraught, and fluid."[39]

For example, missionary practice did not mirror missionary teaching. By the end of the nineteenth century, Progressive American women teaching in Hawai'i were more concerned with class and race than with gender, despite their feminist ideals. Due to their foreign status, American women became accustomed to participating in activities with other *haole* (white residents), as opposed to native Hawaiian women. Conversely, Hawaiian men who converted to Christianity often accepted American racial and gender inequalities in order to participate in American-funded missionary activities throughout the Pacific. Polynesian women, I argue, had different plans altogether.[40]

Racial differences, religious narratives, and nationalist concerns met each other in the Polynesian islands during the nineteenth century, yet the politics of gender ultimately defined how these power dynamics would unfold. British, French, and American patriarchal concepts of gender usurped Polynesian gender systems, including the political leadership of women, and represented a cultural revolution that was as much a tragedy as was the formal colonization of Tahiti and Hawai'i by France and the United States. Further, European and American racism prevented Polynesians from influencing Anglo-European constructs of gender.

The chiefs in these chapters understood the political climate in which they lived and used both Indigenous and foreign approaches to governance in order to maintain their own influence upon international events. The overall objective of these women was to secure independence for themselves and their families and for their islands. In the process they utilized their authority to improve the position of women living in Tahiti and the Hawaiian Islands. On occasion, they also appropriated patriarchal forms of colonial government for their own designs. Unfortunately, the women met resistance at every turn and achieved varying degrees of success.

These successes, however, have been lost in the archives, as imperial histories and missionary accounts dominated by white men chose to tell different stories. Manktelow reminds us that women's history "means giving women's words more weight than they were given at the time in recognition of the power imbalances between the sexes in practice, and the practice of archival documentation."[41] With her end in mind, I hope to re-center the lives of Purea, 'Aimata, Ka'ahumanu, and Lili'uokalani in the historiography of nineteenth-century international relations.

I

@

Purea

Kula i ka nuʻu.
[Strive to reach the highest.]
—HAWAIIAN PROVERB

When Purea was born around the year 1720, her father offered sacrifices to the gods, and a *paia* (priest) buried her naval cord inside the family's *marae* (temple). Like all children born in Tahiti, Purea was sacred, a "child god," her naval cord a sign that she was connected to the gods. Anything Purea touched was rendered forbidden, unable to be used by her family until she had completed all of the necessary religious rites of childhood. In Tahiti a tree would be cut down if a child's head accidentally grazed the branches. For a boy, these ceremonies might take six or seven years to complete. For Purea and other girls, religious rites ended around the age of sixteen or seventeen.[1]

In Tahiti the godhead of children meant that the birth of a genealogically superior child allowed the child to supersede the will of his or her parents. Purea understood this and was able to direct these long-standing cultural traditions in ways that increased her own political power. She did so in the midst of social revolution, instigated by Raiʻatean priests who encouraged allegiance to a new god, Oro, the god of war. When the first Europeans arrived in Tahiti, they did not understand that complicated Tahitian gender systems were already being utilized by Purea to direct the future of Tahiti. They also did not realize that unification through war was an idea largely foreign to Tahitians prior to Purea's political ascendency. What the English sailors sought was a Tahitian leader with whom to negotiate trade—their trinkets for Tahitian food and water. In doing so they unwittingly played into a contest for power that had nothing to do with them.

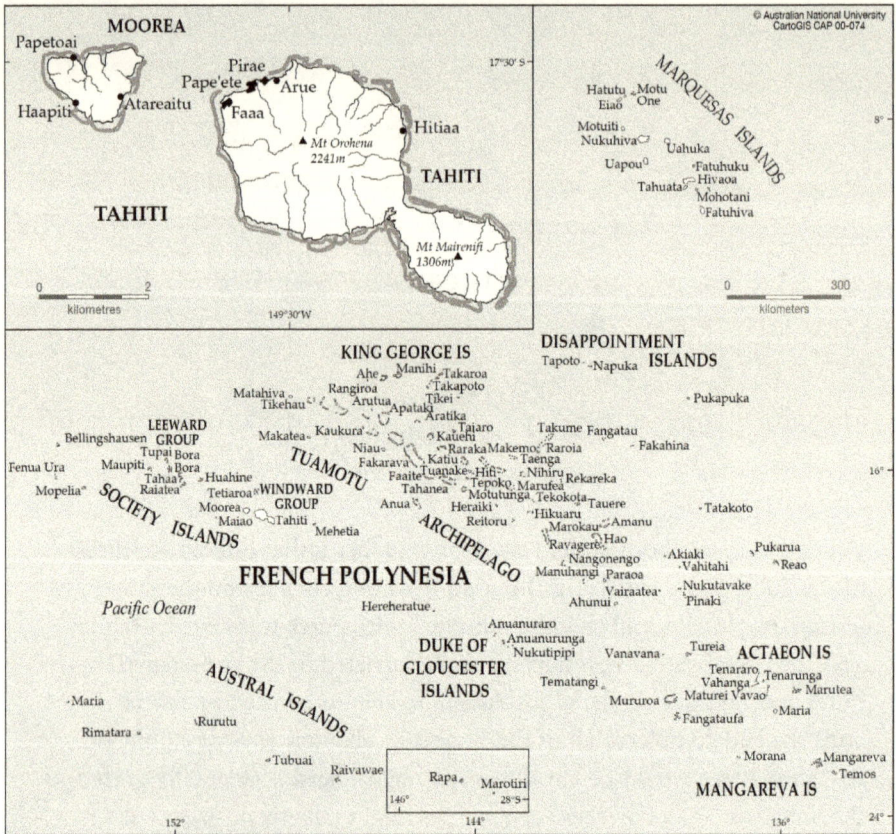

2. French Polynesia. Map reproduced with the permission of
CartoGIS Services, Scholarly Information Services, The Australian
National University, http://asiapacific.anu.edu.au/mapsonline/.

3. (*opposite*) Political districts of Tahiti. Map reproduced with the permission
of CartoGIS Services, Scholarly Information Services, The Australian
National University, http://asiapacific.anu.edu.au/mapsonline/.

Power Politics

Purea's full name was Te vahine Airotua i Ahurai i Farepua, and her lineage
was among the highest in Tahiti. As the firstborn child of the chief of the
Fa'a'ā district, Purea inherited the power and titles of her father and the
royal lineage of her mother, the high chieftainess of Ahurai. At the time of
Purea's birth, the highest chiefs of Tahiti traced their descent back to the
great Tamatoa line of kings on Rai'atea, but no Tahitian chief had been able

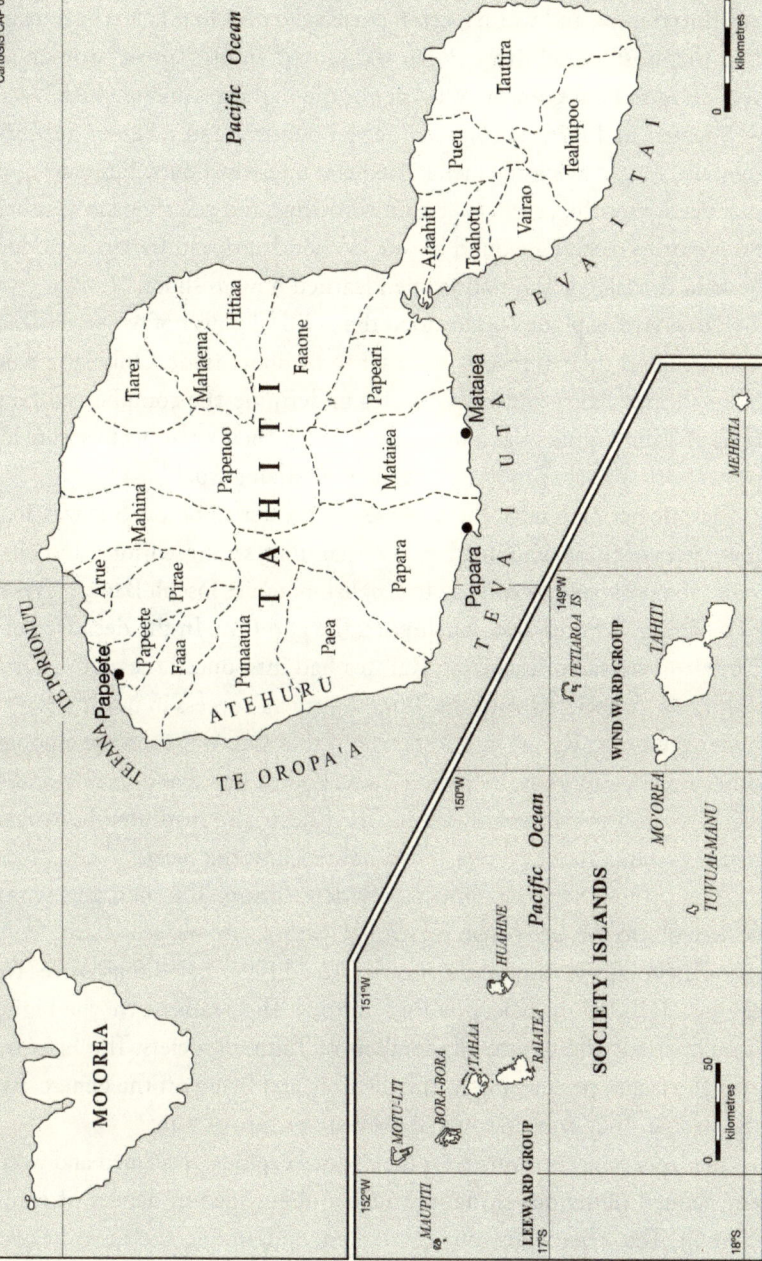

© Australian National University
CartoGIS CAP 00-170

Pacific Ocean

17°30'S

MO'OREA

TE PORIONU'U

Papeete

148°30'W

TE FANA

Arue

Mahina

Pirae

Papeete

Faaa

Punaauia

Paea

Tiarei

Papenoo

Mahaena

Hitiaa

Faaone

T A H I T I

Mataiea

Papeari

Papara

ATEHURU

TE OROPA'A

Papara

Mataiea

TEVA I UTA

Afaahiti

Toahotu

Vairao

Teahupoo

Pueu

Tautira

TEVA I TAI

Pacific Ocean

0   100
kilometres

MEHETIA

149°W

TETIAROA IS

WIND WARD GROUP

TAHITI

MO'OREA

TUTU'AI-MANU

150°W

Pacific Ocean

SOCIETY ISLANDS

151°W

HUAHINE

TAHA'A

RA'IATEA

152°W

MOTU-ITI

BORA-BORA

MAUPITI

LEEWARD GROUP

17°S

18°S

0   50
kilometres

to exert sole power over the island, as had the Tamatoa clan on Rai'atea. In determining rank, matrilineal lines in Tahiti were just as important as patrilineal ones, and women often played the deciding factor in transmitting the most sacred titles. Purea was one of Tahiti's "great" women and, according to Niel Gunson, was "*in fact* the highest-ranking chief."[2]

Women in Tahiti not only conferred political and religious authority; they also fought alongside men in frequent intertribal wars. Tahitian women practiced wrestling, archery, javelin throwing, and the slingshot, "it being no honor to receive a wound in war." When European traders introduced guns to the island, Tahitian women learned how to shoot.[3]

Early naval explorers understood the political power of women in Tahiti and accepted their authority in order to facilitate trade. Only later would English merchants and missionaries undermine the complicated family lines of Tahitian rulers, as a means to simplify their attempts to secure legal protections, private property, and the Christian gospel.[4]

Despite her high rank, Purea possessed greater ambition. She was, in the memories of those who met her, commanding, strong, curious, and observant. She possessed, according to English botanist Joseph Banks, "eyes full of meaning."[5] Purea also worshipped the god Oro. In the decades before European arrival, priests from Rai'atea had introduced the cult of Oro to Tahitians. Associated with the Tamatoa chiefs' success in uniting Rai'atea under their rule, Rai'atean priests taught that Oro was supreme among all other Polynesian gods, including Tane, god of peace and beauty and the principal god worshiped on Tahiti. The priests also instituted human sacrifices and initiated devotees into a new society, the *'arioi*.[6]

As a group the *'arioi* almost defy description. The men and women accepted into the *'arioi* were expert navigators, orators, musicians, "comedians" (actors), warriors, and dancers. *'Arioi* differentiated themselves from the rest of Tahitian society by their tattoos. Their ranks, save the highest, were open for audition to all members of Tahitian society. The *'arioi* traveled the island performing in the districts and living off the generosity of the people. They were untouchable even in times of war.[7]

The *'arioi* were also known for their sexual exploits. *'Arioi* men and women entertained numerous sexual partners and engaged in dances of explicit content. The *'arioi* were young, talented, and among the most beautiful people on the island. Even after leaving the group to establish a home and family, an *'arioi* always retained exalted status.[8]

As a young woman, Purea became an 'arioi. Because of her chiefly status, she also obtained the highest rank of 'arioi, the avioi maro 'ura ("comedian of the red-loin girdle"), red feathers being associated with Oro. Also known as the "black legs," the avioi maro 'ura were identified by the tattoos which ran from their buttocks down to the back of their knees. They were considered the most exclusive group of ari'i (chiefly class) in Tahiti. It was as a black leg that Purea met her future husband, Amo, a fellow black leg, the chief of Papara, and a member of the important Teva clan.[9]

Because of their transient and indulgent lifestyles, as well as their emphasis on physical beauty (marred, they believed, by breastfeeding), the 'arioi forbade parenthood. 'Arioi men and women were required to strangle their newborn children or leave the society. As one missionary observed, "Players who became parents [were] a distinct class of 'arioi. They were made distinct because they were parents and saved the lives of their progeny. Therefore, they were [disenfranchised]." 'Arioi parents could no longer enjoy the benefits of 'arioi society nor associate with other 'arioi, save those who had become parents. The missionary put it bluntly: "The Player may be a whoremonger at pleasure and have many children, so long as he does not have one alive."[10]

Purea and Amo's marriage in the mid-eighteenth century did not preclude maintaining their status as black legs. In fact, the couple's power grew. By combining their landholdings, Purea and Amo controlled most of the western and southern districts of Tahiti. With no children they retained all political and sacred titles associated with their status. Only an infant could stand in their way.[11]

A Son Is Born

In 1762 Purea became pregnant. Purea had been pregnant before and had allowed others to kill her newborn children, but the 'arioi custom was not absolute. As one inhabitant noted, "If the child should chance to cry out in coming into the world, or should the mother chance to see it before it is killed, nature takes place of custom, and the child is saved." Purea already had gone through childbirth, perhaps as many as nine times, but this time was different. Purea delivered the baby alone, and because she saw him and heard him cry, she let the child live.[12]

Purea named the child Teri'irere and, in that moment, determined to exert her enormous ambition and political strength into making her son the king of Tahiti, god-child of Oro, in the tradition of the Tamatoa kings on Rai'atea, a feat no Tahitian had yet accomplished.[13]

Purea's decision set in motion a series of events that would alter the Pacific world. Purea's husband Amo was furious with her decision. Both Purea and Amo lost their sacred positions as *arioi* once they became parents, but, more importantly, Amo lost his political power as well. As one Tahitian mother explained, "The son always superseded the father, whose authority after the birth of a child was merely that of a guardian."[14]

Amo refused to live with Purea after Teri'irere's birth, but because Purea was the highest-ranking chief on the island, her wishes for her son dictated the terms of Amo's regency, and her governance in Teri'irere's life was more involved than a Tahitian mother's influence over her son traditionally would be.[15]

Purea's plan was ingenious. She and Amo would construct a new *marae* in the district of Papara, and it would be the largest sacred site on the island. There, with the aid of an Oro priest, Purea and Amo would install their son with the *maro 'ura* (red feather girdle)—similar to ones they had worn symbolically as *arioi*, but in this case it could be worn politically only by an *ari'i nui* (royal chief). The couple would also gift their son the *maro tea* (yellow feather girdle), which only the Teva grand chief of Papara could wear. No one in Tahiti had ever worn the two girdles at the same time, and by consecrating Teri'irere with both girdles, Purea intended to declare her son *ari'i rahi* (paramount chief of Tahiti).[16]

Purea ordered the *manahune* (people) of Papara to begin construction on the *marae*, the remains of which the botanist Joseph Banks later called "the masterpiece of [Polynesian] architecture in this island." Constructed with coral stone, the edifice measured over forty feet high and seventy feet wide and was nearly the size of a football field in length. Banks marveled at the symmetry of the stones, cut without iron implements and assembled without mortar.[17]

Purea also ordered a *rahui* (eating taboo). A *rahui* was a prohibition against consuming anything produced on the land during the duration of the taboo. All was to be considered sacred and belonging to the chief, in this case, the young Teri'irere. Purea intended to end the *rahui* at a great feast in the new *marae* to celebrate her son's investiture with the red and yellow girdles. A *rahui* could last many months and produce great hardship for the people. Purea's *rahui* for her son extended across the island and caused disruption among other chiefs, who attempted to break the *rahui* by traveling to see Purea. According to tradition, a chief of equal rank could break *rahui* by imposing on a chief's generosity. In other words, Purea would be forced to end the *rahui* in order to house and feed her guests.[18]

The first person to attempt to break the *rahui* was Purea's sister-in-law, sailing from Fa'a'ā on a royal barge with fifty men. Purea's niece was next. As one descendant recalled, Purea's *rahui* was "more than Purea's female relations could bear, and it set society in a ferment." In each encounter, Purea turned the chiefs away and refused to acknowledge their equality. Purea refused to break her *rahui*. "How many more royal heads can there be?" Purea asked. "I know none but Teri'irere." In both her declaration of the *rahui* and her refusal to entertain her extended family, Purea declared she and her son the supreme rulers of Tahiti. Into this tense and contested political dynamic the first Europeans arrived.[19]

First English Encounter

When English captain Samuel Wallis and his crew on the HMS *Dolphin* first spotted the island of Tahiti on June 19, 1767, Wallis and many of his men were dangerously sick with scurvy. The men were charged by King George III to circumnavigate the earth for only the second time in British history, and the *Dolphin* had been at sea for almost a year before it anchored in Matavai Bay. Wallis's secret orders were to search for a southern continent, rumored to lie within the Pacific Ocean. Ostensibly sailing for scientific purposes, Wallis was also charged with securing superior trading rights along the way, even colonizing land for such purposes. By the time the *Dolphin*'s crew sighted Tahiti, Wallis and his sailors badly needed fresh water, produce, and solid ground upon which to recover their health. The Tahitian people did not intend to allow the English to land.[20]

Tahitians already were familiar with non-Polynesian exploration as the result of a Dutch ship, the *Afrikaansche Galei*, which had sunk nearby many decades before. Although they were able to procure very little from the wreck, the Tahitians found small amounts of iron nails, which they realized could supplement the pounded pearl and tortoise shells they used as fish hooks and the tar from breadfruit trees they used for canoe pitch. Wallis instructed his men to be ready to trade trinkets for food, and the *Dolphin*'s crew held out nails and beads, as scores of canoes surrounded the ship, and thousands of Tahitians watched from the shore. From their canoes the Tahitians offered pigs, breadfruit, bananas, apples, plantains, and mangoes.[21]

At the same time, several men from the *Dolphin* took a small cutter toward shore in an attempt to find a spot for sailors to land. They were turned back forcefully by Tahitian warriors in canoes. As the Tahitian warriors became more aggressive, the British sailors fired. One warrior was injured; another was killed.[22]

Over the next several days, members of the *Dolphin*'s crew attempted to acquire fresh water, but the Tahitians, amassing on the beach, refused to allow them to land. The crew fired their guns into the air in protest and prepared their ship for a Tahitian assault. On June 24 Tahitian warriors aboard more than three hundred canoes attacked the *Dolphin*. The British released their cannon directly into the oncoming fleet, killing many warriors. On June 25 Wallis, too weak with scurvy to go ashore, ordered his lieutenant to raise a red pennant on the beach and declare Tahiti a British possession.[23]

Wallis renamed the island "King George's Island." On June 26 Tahitian warriors made one more attempt to attack the British, who, this time, fired onto land. From that point forward, Wallis's men simply pointed their muskets at the Tahitians or shot into the air to enforce what the British believed was fair trade. To prevent additional attacks, the *Dolphin*'s crew also tore apart nearly one hundred Tahitian canoes, some large enough to hold thirty people. "The islanders," Anne Salmond writes, "saw the first Europeans who visited Tahiti as terrifying beings who blew into their weapons, making them thunder and flash and hurl stones that killed many people."[24]

Her Majesty

Despite the English show of force, Purea determined to visit the *Dolphin*. A member of Wallis's crew was the first to notice Purea walking on the beach several days after the destruction, noting in his journal that he had observed "a fine well look[ing] woman of [dark color], with a great many men along with her who seemed to pay her a great deal of respect." Wallis greeted Purea when she climbed aboard the *Dolphin* with her retinue on July 13. The captain recorded that Purea "was quite free and easy on her coming aboard and all the time she was there." Purea, Wallis noted, was a "tall, well-looking woman about forty-five years old, and paid great respect by the inhabitants."[25]

Purea invited Wallis to shore, and the next day the captain left the ship for the first time since its arrival in Tahiti, visiting Purea's "large house," filled with guards and servants and surrounded by "a multitude of people." Inside the house Purea ordered several young girls to massage Wallis and two of his sick officers. Purea presented Wallis with a pregnant sow and walked with him back to the ship. When reaching an area of wetlands, Purea carried Wallis across. "She took me by the arm and lifted me over every slough with as much ease as I could (when in health) a child," Wallis marveled. Thereafter, Wallis referred to Purea as "the queen."[26]

Purea likely traveled to Matavai Bay as soon as she heard about the strange visitors. During the *Dolphin*'s stay, Amo, Purea's husband, did not appear, although Tahitian oral tradition records that he was hiding nearby in the woods. Consequently, Purea appeared to Wallis as sole ruler of the Tahitian people, an impression Purea used to her advantage. Wallis described each of his visits with Purea but made critical errors in interpreting those events. Complicating the record further, Wallis added to his journal stories relayed to him by crewmembers who had gone ashore during the time he remained sick in his cabin.[27]

For example, Wallis gave sole responsibility for negotiating terms of trade with the Tahitian people to his gunner, Harrison, who was invited to attend a large feast hosted by Purea. Harrison reported to Wallis that as many as one thousand people were present. Based upon Harrison's account, Wallis recorded that Purea "gave to everyone a mess from her own hands" before allowing herself to be fed by two servants. Harrison's account signaled to Wallis that Purea was a commanding leader, "a queen," whose generosity would facilitate trade relations between the British and Tahitians and, more importantly, would save the lives of his crew. "From this day [we] never wanted a fresh meal all the while we stayed here," Wallis noted.[28]

What Wallis did not record nor could he have known was the meaning behind what Harrison witnessed. As later English visitors, including Captain Cook, would learn, Purea's "prodigious" house was not actually her own, nor did she live in the district in which the *Dolphin* had landed. Rather than simple generosity, Purea was in the process of consolidating her son's power across the island, using the local meeting house as her staging ground, and viewing the superiority of British cannons and guns, not as a sign of defeat, but as an opportunity to strengthen her authority over the Tahitian people.[29]

George Robertson, a midshipman aboard the *Dolphin*, gives further clues to the motivation behind Purea's actions. As Wallis made his first visit to shore, Purea gathered the people around her on the beach and "made a long speech to them," Robertson noticed. "All the people gave great attention, not a whisper was heard while she spoke." After finishing her speech, Purea pointed to Wallis and his officers and "made her people understand that they were the principle people belonging to the ship."[30]

Later that day Purea sent to the ship more pigs, fowl, and fruit than the crew had been able to collect from the Tahitian people during all of the previous three days. During Wallis's next visit to shore, Purea tied red feathers in his hair.[31]

These journal entries are remarkable for what they suggest. In offering the people a feast and gifting red feathers to Wallis, Purea was embarking into uncharted political territory and perhaps breaking her own *rahui*. By feeding the *Dolphin*'s crew and continuing to supply them with a steady stream of food, Purea was declaring that the foreigners were her political equals and worthy of hospitality, a statement demonstrated by her gift of red feathers to Wallis, a color which, the captain noted, only Purea wore.[32]

Bounty mutineer James Morrison later recorded that long speeches, large feasts, and gifts of pigs, palm branches, and red feathers for one's ear or hair were symbols of peace offered by a chief to a visiting chief of equal rank. That Purea could offer so much livestock to the *Dolphin*'s crew was because, quite possibly, it already had been held back for her son, a cultural practice Wallis did not understand and a misunderstanding that would affect the trade efforts of future naval ships seeking to restock on "King George's Island."[33]

Purea also appears to have broken an even older Tahitian prohibition. Tahitian men and women ate separately. For example, women were never allowed to feast with men in a *marae* or at a political ceremony. In domestic life husbands and wives retained separate cooking huts. Men were forbidden to handle a woman's food or cooking utensil, although a woman could provide food to a man. By gathering the people together and serving them her own food, Purea declared that she held the highest status on the island, as a woman was never allowed to eat in the presence of a man of superior rank. Purea was establishing her ability to define Tahitian prohibitions and freedoms, a privilege highly contested by other chiefs and family members in Tahiti.[34]

When Purea fed the people, she demonstrated her womanhood by not touching what a man had touched, while also asserting before all the men present that she held the highest chiefly status in Tahiti. In requiring two women to feed her, Purea also maintained that her *ari'i rahi* status was sacred, given directly to her by Oro. Each of these actions established for the people that Purea *alone* defined sacred and political law for the island, a responsibility she planned to share with her son by appointing him with the red and yellow girdles when he reached puberty.[35]

Purea's vision never came to fruition. On one of his last visits to shore, Wallis, through his gestures and attempts at communication, announced that the *Dolphin* would be leaving. Purea understood and wept. Much would later be made of her reaction by readers in England, but neither British romantics nor imperialists realized what Purea's weeping actually meant. Without Wallis or his crew, Purea unlikely would be able to defend her brilliant but dangerous political plan. Over the following days Purea begged Wallis to stay, yet on July 29 Wallis and the *Dolphin* left Matavai Bay and Purea's tears behind.[36]

War

Purea might never have attempted to secure political power over the districts of Tahiti if she had not given birth to a son. The only previous example of island unification had come from Rai'atea, where kings achieved power through both war and maternal lines. Knowledge of such power had been brought by Rai'atean priests who were men. Because Tahitian women were restricted from conducting *marae* rites, Purea's attempts to institute a new religion and secure political allegiance from each district under the threat of war likely would have been impossible without the regency she established over her son.

Only one person in Tahiti could legitimately challenge the lineage of Purea and Amo's son for the position of *ari'i rahi*, and after the British left, he did. Tu, the high chief of the northern district of Arue, was the son of Tetupaia, the daughter and eldest child of king Tamatoa III of Rai'atea. Tu's matrilineal descent linked him directly to the chiefly line of Rai'atea. Some chiefs argued that Tu held the more important link to Rai'atea. Additionally, Tetupaia's uncle was Tamatoa I, whereas Purea's son claimed his connection to Rai'atea only through Tamatoa I's widow. Tu's regent and great uncle, Tutaha, believed Tu was the rightful one to rule a unified Tahiti.[37]

4. Purea's gift of breadfruit palms was a symbol of peace, not surrender, in this misappropriated title, *The Surrender of the Island of Otaheite to Captain Wallis by the Supposed Queen Oberea*. John Hall, 1773. © National Maritime Museum, Greenwich, London.

Purea's attempts to unite Tahiti spectacularly backfired for her but ultimately succeeded for her rivals. In December 1768, fifteen months after the *Dolphin* left Tahiti, Tutaha organized a coalition of chiefs and warriors to attack Papara, dismantle Purea's *marae*, and steal the red and yellow girdles meant for Teri'irere. The "*Rahui* War" was a disaster for Purea and the people of Papara. Purea, Amo, and Teri'irere fled to the mountains as Purea's enemies massacred her people and left their bodies strewn across the beach. According to an ancient song sung in Papara, Purea and Amo were attacked at their son's investiture ceremony by the chiefs whom they had invited.[38]

Purea surrendered. Although her son was allowed to retain the yellow *maro* and his position as chief of Papara, Tutaha and his coalition invested Tu with the red *maro*. While not all Tahitian chiefs accepted Tu's kingship, or the idea of an *ari'i rahi*, Tu, as Pōmare I, would use the title to solidify his kingship, not in the eyes of his people, but in the eyes of the Europeans.[39]

After the English came the French, Spanish, and Americans. By the early nineteenth century, the British government had secured a trade agreement with Tu, and the British governor of Australia could write that Tahiti was "the only island that needs little or no precaution for the safety of those who visit it." Tahitians understood that ships brought trade goods, and Tu understood that his monopoly on trade brought political power. Consequently, the British colonial office devised a plan to run pigs from Tahiti to Australia to feed the British convicts forced to migrate to the southern continent.[40]

European ships also brought sailors with false conceptions of Tahitian promiscuity and submissiveness. The effects were manifold. The first women whom the *Dolphin*'s crew witnessed were *'arioi* warriors in war canoes. Their sexual gestures and pantomimes were titillating to the sailors but actually constituted acts of violence to the Tahitians. As the Tahitians prepared to attack the visitors, the *'arioi* women attempted to strip the white men of their *mana*, or power. Tahitians believed the ability to take a man's *mana* rested uniquely with a woman through the use of her sexuality. As Noenoe Silva explains, the concept of *mana* "require[ed] practice and a certain kind of follow-up with action."[41]

Similar misconceptions arose when Tahitian women appeared naked in public. European men again mistook (perhaps not inadvertently) their nudity as promiscuity. The Tahitian women who exposed their breasts, however, were in the presence of an *ari'i*, such as Purea. Whenever a Tahitian chief was present, all men and women of lower status were required to strip to their waists. Unfortunately, the English sailors accepted these cultural practices as evidence that Tahitian women were willing to become their sexual partners, a belief that Tahitians soon utilized to their trade advantage. As one sailor noticed: "The old men made [the girls] stand in rank, and made signs for our people to take which they liked best." As the crew begged their captain to allow the girls aboard, the sailor observed, "the poor young girls seemed a little afraid."[42]

As sailors aboard the *Dolphin* traded iron for sex, inflation on the value of a nail quadrupled. So many nails were traded by the sailors for sex that men took out the nails from their own hammocks and slept on the deck. When the officer in charge of trade relations with the Tahitians tried to address the overall trade deficit, he found the other officers unwilling to interfere, as they, too, were engaged in their own private trade. It's unclear what Captain Wallis would have done if he had been in better health. Wallis remained unaware of the extent of these activities for most of the *Dolphin's* stay. As a result, the sailors introduced venereal disease to the Tahitians.[43]

David Igler has argued that the trade relationship between native men and white men often placed Polynesian women into a position of forced prostitution, a concept and occupation previously unknown in Polynesia. Prior to European arrival, the only class of Tahitians regularly to engage in promiscuity was the highest chiefly class, such as the *'arioi*. After European arrival, Tahitian women began to suffer the catastrophic effects of syphilis, including sterility, miscarriage, and high infant mortality.[44]

Tahitians suffered from other infectious diseases as well. French ships brought an epidemic in 1770, and smallpox was transported by an American ship in 1842. It is difficult to know the exact impact that deadly diseases had upon the Tahitian population, since early population estimates by European visitors varied widely. But English mutineer James Morrison, who lived on the island in the early 1790s, estimated the population of Tahiti to be around thirty thousand. The first census, conducted by English missionaries in 1802, revealed that the Tahitian population had fallen to six thousand, a decline of 80 percent. Such a dramatic decrease in population due to the introduction of foreign diseases would be in line with similar events on other Pacific islands.[45]

Legacies

Purea unconsciously added to European misconceptions of Tahitian lasciviousness. Once English military superiority had been demonstrated to her, Purea personally targeted *Dolphin* crewmember George Robertson for a sexual liaison, most probably to join the English and Tahitian genealogical lines through procreation, an acceptable practice for men and women of chiefly status. When Robertson showed Purea that he could lift her with one arm and carry her around the room, she was astounded, introducing him to family members and other chiefs. Purea then attempted to lift Robertson but could not. Appearing satisfied, Purea presented Robertson to the Tahitian people, who were, in his words, "extremely well pleased." From that point forward Purea harshly rebuked any young woman who

5. *A Young Woman of Otaheite Bringing a Present,* by Francesco Bartolozzi, 1784. This engraving is based upon a drawing by John Webber, who accompanied Captain Cook on his third voyage. The elaborate ceremony included a girl lifting up her skirt while standing on her gift of tapa cloth. National Library of Australia.

approached Robertson, and Captain Wallis observed that the ship received "more stock than any day yet" after Robertson's liaison with Purea.[46]

One might be tempted to view Purea's physical tests and displays of jealousy as humorous, but to the Tahitians, they were life, power, and legacy. These behaviors also make sense of a story Robertson relates about a young

Tahitian woman who went to great lengths to rid herself of her husband in order to have sex with a member of the *Dolphin*'s crew. While Robertson believed the woman to be infatuated with the sailor, it is more likely that the woman was attempting to join herself with the Englishman's *mana*. What is tragic about the anecdote is that if the woman's husband had discovered her actions, he, by custom, could have killed her.[47]

English hubris regarding the tantalizing playground of Tahiti reached its zenith under the auspices of Joseph Banks. The wealthy English botanist paid his own way to Tahiti, accompanying Captain Cook aboard the *Endeavor* on Cook's first voyage across the Pacific. Ostensibly traveling to measure the transit of Venus from the position of Tahiti, Cook also intended to continue exploration of the Pacific Ocean for the royal navy. As Banks prepared to depart with Cook and his crew, the botanist boasted to friends about "the excellent opportunity I now ha[ve] to improve science and achieve fame."[48]

The *Endeavor* arrived in Tahiti in 1769, and Banks kept a detailed journal of his experiences on the island. Banks collected flora and fauna, took a Tahitian lover, and traveled with Cook to the district of Papara to see the remains of Purea's *marae*. Banks also met Purea. Not impressed by the "*Dolphin*'s queen," Banks concluded that Purea "might have been handsome when young, but now few or no traces of it were left." Banks also boasted that Purea had propositioned him for sex more than once, but he had refused her.[49]

Banks's flippant remarks had repercussions back home. The English public viewed the voyages of the *Dolphin* and *Endeavor* as scientific missions, an interpretation the Admiralty fueled by funding the 1773 publication of a compilation of journals from four English captains: Byron, Carteret, Wallis, and Cook. With the approval of King George III, the Royal Navy chose John Hawkesworth to weave the journals into a narrative and paid six thousand pounds to him in advance to do so, the largest sum paid to an author by an English publisher during the eighteenth century. Hawkesworth decided to include Banks's journal in the project.[50]

While today the name of Captain Cook is well known, in the eighteenth century Joseph Banks was the hero upon the *Endeavor*'s return to England in 1771. Captain Cook immediately began to prepare for his second voyage, but Banks became the toast of London, using his invitations and speeches to secure a position as president of the Royal Society of London for Improving Natural Knowledge (the Royal Society), a position he held for forty years.

Banks's two primary contributions to the Society during his tenure were to recommend that Australia become the new home for English, Irish, and Scottish convicts and to suggest that transplanted Tahitian breadfruit trees would provide cheap food for British Caribbean slaves. His latter proposal led to the infamous voyage of Captain Bligh aboard the HMS *Bounty* in 1787. After leaving Tahiti with a cargo of breadfruit trees, members of the *Bounty*'s crew mutinied against Bligh, returned to Tahiti to kidnap several Tahitian women, and took them to Pitcairn Island, where the men established a community that still exists today.[51]

During the drafting of his manuscript, Hawkesworth was in constant communication with Banks. It appears the author had little contact with the British captains, however, as two of the four later complained about inaccuracies in the published version. Most controversially, Hawkesworth decided to combine the five journals into one first-person narrative. "It was readily acknowledged on all hands that a narrative in the first person would ... more strongly incite an interest, and consequently afford more entertainment," Hawkesworth explained.[52]

The decision to combine accounts would later haunt Hawkesworth, as shocked readers blamed the author for so vigilantly reporting the sexual encounters recorded by Banks and the captains during their voyages. Believing his reputation ruined, Hawkesworth fell into a deep depression and died less than a year later. An outraged public did not mean that the book was a failure, however. The manuscript, published as *An Account of the Voyages Undertaken by the Order of His Present Majesty for Making Discoveries in the Southern Hemisphere, and Successively Performed by Commodore Byron, Captain Carteret, Captain Wallis, and Captain Cook, in the* Dolphin, *the* Swallow, *and the* Endeavor: *Drawn Up from the Journals which were Kept by the Several Commanders, and from the Papers of Joseph Banks, Esq., by John Hawkesworth, LL.D. in Three Volumes*, was an instant bestseller and translated into at least three languages. Most importantly, it was the public's first formal introduction to the people of Tahiti.[53]

Hawkesworth took many sentimental liberties in copying the journals, a decision to which he freely admitted in his introduction to the second volume. "Captain Cook from the Admiralty, was obliging as to put it into my hands, with permission to take out of it whatever I thought would improve or embellish the narrative," Hawkesworth wrote. "This was an offer of which I gladly and thankfully accepted."[54]

Two of Hawkesworth's most significant liberties came from Wallis's journal and involved Purea. In his own journal, which was not published until 2016, Wallis recorded on July 14: "I went on shore for the first time where the queen I may call her soon came." Instead, Hawkesworth translated the passage, "I went on shore for the first time where my Princess, or rather queen . . . soon after came to me." The intended effect on the reader is obvious. Wallis was smitten, and so was Purea.[55]

On the day of the *Dolphin*'s departure, Wallis wrote with similar succinctness: "At ten a breeze sprang up, and we took leave of the Queen and all our worthy friends." Hawkesworth, however, added to the captain's version: "A fresh breeze springing up, our Indian friends, and particularly the queen, once more bade us farewell, with such tenderness of affection and grief, as filled both my heart and my eyes."[56]

English readers went wild over the thought of an English sea captain weeping at the loss of his Tahitian princess. Conservative politicians steamed, Protestant ministers worried, and forward-thinking brothels rebranded. One such establishment advertised in the *Whoremongers Guide to London* that twelve virgins would "carry out the feast of Venus, as it is celebrated in Tahiti, under the instruction and leadership of Queen Oberea [Purea]." The brothel's owner, a woman, announced that she would play the part of Purea.[57]

Because neither Captains Wallis nor Cook published their own accounts of their voyages, Hawkesworth's melodramatic prose describing the first English encounters with the Tahitian people provided the English people with their first glimpses of Polynesia. Hawkesworth's decision to include Banks's journal also led to Banks's rapid social rise and the consequent emergence of detractors. Soon satirical pamphlets appeared in the British press, making ribald fun of the botanist's sexual exploits in Tahiti.[58] Published anonymously, these tracts also defamed Purea. One, titled *An Epistle from Oberea, Queen of Otaheite, to Joseph Banks, Esq., Translated by T.Q.Z. Esq., Professor of the Otaheite Language in Dublin, and of all the Language of the Undiscovered Islands in the South Sea*, opined:

> I, *Oberea*, from the Southern main,
> Of flighted vows, of injured faith complain.
> Though now some European maid you woo,
> Of waist more taper, and of whiter hue;

> Yet oft with me you deigned the night to pass,
> Beneath yon bread-tree on the bending grass.[59]

Banks's playful descriptions of Purea's supposed desire for him resulted in Purea becoming a farce. By treating Purea as an anthropological subject, Banks reduced her to a member of a primitive society that needed transformation under the guiding authority of the British Empire. Elites who read Hawkesworth or met Banks came to believe that Tahiti possessed a valuable economy in want of British control due to the island's moral failure of excess that had allowed its women to dictate the terms of trade by using their sexual and political *mana*.[60]

Conclusion

Hawkesworth's account of early English voyages to Tahiti left English readers caught between projecting their "desires and fears" onto a people they believed to be racially inferior. The English public vacillated in their opinions. John Wesley, a Methodist minister and influential leader in the Second Great Awakening, was scandalized by Hawkesworth's account. "Men and women coupling together in the face of the sun, and in the sight of scores of people!" he exclaimed. English revivalists immediately began plans to send missionaries to Tahiti. Others in English society mustered only enough moral courage to condemn Hawkesworth's book in anonymous letters written to the press.[61]

One way a person could resolve the perceived contradiction between the sexual promiscuity and political power of Tahitian women was to assume that Tahitian women such as Purea were *too* free and *too* aggressive. Therefore, Tahiti remained *too* far removed from England in its stage of civilization to preclude Britain's control of the island. Such were the inconsistencies of Enlightenment progress. Why shouldn't the British Empire absorb so wanton a place as one ruled by a sex-crazed despot who pined for an Englishman? Hawkesworth already had argued as much when he expressed regret for the natives who had been killed by Wallis's men but concluded that the affair "appears to be an evil which, if discoveries of new countries are attempted, cannot be avoided."[62]

The irony of such conclusions is that the British government did not intend to rule the island. The Admiralty had instructed Wallis to trade, not

obereyaa Enchantress

6. In London Purea became a popular representation of Tahitian royalty
and sensuality. Costume design for "Obereyaa the Enchantress" by
Philip James de Loutherbourg for *Omai*, a London pantomime about
Tahiti and Captain Cook (1785). National Library of Australia.

7. Purea as Eve, the "temptress." From a limited-print edition of *An Epistle from Oberea, Queen of Otaheite, to Joseph Banks, Esq.*, originally published in London in 1774. Original artwork by Australian artist Ray Crooke for Rams Skull Press, 1955. Courtesy of David Crooke.

conquer. "You are moreover to endeavor to make purchases and with the consent of the Inhabitants—take possession of convenient situations—in the country in the name of the King of Great Britain," the Admiralty's instructions to Wallis read. "But if no inhabitants are found on the land or islands discovered, you are, in such case, to take possession of such lands or islands for His Majesty by setting up proper marks and inscriptions as first discoverers and possessors."[63]

Wallis may have staked a red English pennant on Tahiti in 1767, but it meant little other than satisfaction for him and his crew. In the coming years both France and Spain would also lay claims to the island. And as with everything else about the first English-Tahitian encounter, Wallis's gesture had unintended consequences. Within days of his lieutenant staking the red pennant in Tahitian ground, the pennant disappeared. Purea had sewn it into her son's red feather *maro*. As Kathleen Wilson asks about such cross-cultural encounters, "Who is the explorer and who the explored?" By the end of the following year, Tu possessed the red pennant *maro*, and when Cook arrived in Tahiti for the third time in 1778, the people told him Purea was dead.[64]

Although Purea never accomplished what she intended for her family, Purea promoted peaceful trade with Europeans, influenced the emergence of global trade networks, elevated the status of her political rule, and inadvertently laid the groundwork for her rivals to unify Tahiti. While she cannot be considered a monarch like Tu and his Pōmare successors became, Purea politically achieved more than any Tahitian before her had even attempted.

2

'Aimata

Hā'awe i ke kua; hi'i i kea lo.
[A burden on the back; a babe in the arms.]
—HAWAIIAN PROVERB

Between the 1773 publication of Hawkesworth's account of early British voyages to Tahiti and the 1827 crowning of Tahiti's first queen, many changes occurred on the island that aided the ascension of a woman to the Tahitian throne but also hindered her long-term success. British conceptual demands that the government conduct trade diplomacy with a "monarch" had aided Tu in becoming the first Tahitian to be recognized by the British navy as king of the island, yet as Pōmare I, Tu was unable to consolidate his rule over all of Tahiti. The first English missionaries, who arrived in the 1790s, also worked diligently to support the Pōmare clan in its attempts to unify the islands, although it would be another two decades before they would see a Pōmare chief convert to Christianity.

In their efforts to unite Tahitian society under the Pōmares, the missionaries inadvertently paved the way for a Tahitian queenship, yet the religious message they brought prescribed strict gender rules for her. 'Aimata, who would become Queen Pōmare IV, resisted the missionaries' teachings but accepted their aid in establishing her throne. Through much turmoil 'Aimata succeeded in her own political designs until faced with the impenetrable ultimatums of transoceanic imperial powers, which turned their own missionaries' gender prescripts against her continued rule.

Treasured Eye

Named for a high chief who is presented the treasured eye of a sacrificial victim, 'Aimata ("Eye Eater") represented better than any Tahitian chief before her the merging of two worlds: an island transformed by the power of Oro, war, and human sacrifice, and one enticed by the message of Jesus Christ. When ʻAimata was two years old, her father King Pōmare II sent her the gift of an English primer. The king had left his daughter on Tahiti while he fled to nearby Moʻorea. Pōmare was in the midst of war against his enemies on Tahiti, yet the king intended that his daughter should learn the English language while he was away.[1]

Missionaries from the London Missionary Society (LMS) had taught Pōmare II to read and write in the Tahitian language, which the missionaries transcribed for the first time. In his attempt to secure power over Tahiti, Pōmare also adopted the missionaries' religion. Under the guise of Christianity, Pōmare ordered the destruction of all of the idols on Tahiti, thus ensuring that enemy clans could not take their gods into battle against him. By the end of 1815, Pōmare had defeated his enemies and successfully united Tahiti and Moʻorea. In 1819, under the advisement of the missionaries, the king adopted a written code of laws based upon the Bible.[2]

ʻAimata, however, never learned to read or write the Tahitian language, nor did she speak English. Rather than adopt the ways of the missionaries like her father, ʻAimata followed the native path of Purea, who had ruled sixty years before. ʻAimata fiercely defended her Indigenous culture and chiefly status until those efforts cost her the island.[3]

Illegitimate Ruler

When ʻAimata became queen in 1827, she was fourteen years old. Described as lively and free-spirited by the English missionaries, ʻAimata was not the missionaries' first choice to rule the islands. Since 1796, when the first LMS missionaries arrived in the Society Islands, the missionaries had labored with few rewards. Much of the LMS correspondence between the thirty-six missionaries in the islands and their directors in London dealt with the missionaries' lack of basic necessities, requests for higher salaries, concern for the future of their own children, and frustrations with Pōmare II's monopoly on trade, which restricted their buying power. The missionaries hoped that Pōmare's heir, Teriʻitaria, would become the solution to their emigrant problems.[4]

Teriʻitaria was the second child of Pōmare II, but the king had made it clear that his firstborn, ʻAimata, was his wife's child by another man and was not eligible to inherit the throne. When Pōmare II died in 1821,

Teri'itaria was only eighteen months old, yet the missionaries raised the boy with high hopes. When Teri'itaria died of dysentery only six years later, the missionaries were devastated, forced to look to 'Aimata to keep Tahiti and Mo'orea unified. Unfortunately for the missionaries, 'Aimata proved to be a half-hearted partner.[5]

Even at her coronation 'Aimata represented transnational conflict. Unlike her father, who had taken the red *malo* (cloth) from his father as the symbol of *ari'i rahi* status, 'Aimata received a crown and the title "Queen Pōmare IV" from the English missionaries. 'Aimata understood that the missionaries had helped her father consolidate power. In encouraging the king not to kill war captives or plunder his enemies' property, the missionaries aided Pōmare II in securing the acquiescence of rival chiefs. By participating in a Christian coronation, 'Aimata seemed to accept the missionaries' continued involvement in her own island governance, which included her cooperation with the To'ohitu, a court of seven high chiefs created by the missionaries to enforce the newly codified Tahitian laws.[6]

This did not mean that 'Aimata accepted the Christian religion, and several years passed during which 'Aimata demonstrated her defiance of it. Jacques-Antonine Moerenhout, the French consul to Tahiti, noted that 'Aimata brought back many traditional Tahitian dances and songs that the missionaries considered "obscene." Tahitian women, who had been prevented by the missionaries from going aboard European ships, "went there now in troops, accompanying the young queen on her visits." Moerenhout refused to elaborate on these ship parties, writing that the details "would scandalize the reader."[7]

'Aimata's love of entertainment and ancient Tahitian practices included surrounding herself with *faarearea*, girls who devoted themselves to music and dance. The *faarearea* also embraced the sexual promiscuity that had been prevalent among the ancient 'arioi class, and some missionaries believed that 'Aimata had contracted syphilis.[8]

'Aimata also welcomed alternative theologies. "Her court was a virtual center of [Tahitian] resistance to missionary teaching," Niel Gunson writes. 'Aimata was attracted to the Mamaia prophets, who toured the islands during the 1820s. The Mamaia ("fallen fruit") preached their visions of a return to the old ways and gods, including Oro. They questioned the compulsory tithes required by the missionaries and called themselves incarnations of Jesus. The Mamaia preached a hybrid faith that favored Tahitian practices and ridiculed the English, monogamous marriage, and the law. So powerful was the influence of the Mamaia that one missionary called 'Aimata's residence "an abode of infamy."[9] Another missionary recorded in 1828: "There never was a period in which [the Tahitians] manifested such a desire to return to their former customs, as they do at present. In this they are encouraged by the Royal family."[10]

While 'Aimata may have accepted in principle the laws established by her father in 1819, she did not submit willingly to them. Several times 'Aimata found herself close to war with those chiefs who used the To'ohitu court to strengthen their own power. 'Aimata's acceptance of this chiefly court proved complicated. By appointing high-ranking chiefs with judicial authority over the Tahitian people, the missionaries, in effect, diluted the Tahitian monarch's power. In the case of 'Aimata, the court, selected from a list of men, also weakened her political power as a woman. Yet 'Aimata saw a use for the court. She was able to appoint chiefs who might conspire against her into leadership positions that gave the men prominence but also checked their individual schemes. In these contests between her queenship and the law, 'Aimata chose the side that would best maintain her *ari'i rahi* status, playing the rule of law against her enemies or, conversely, defying it for her own purposes.[11]

'Aimata's first confrontation with the high chiefs of Tahiti occurred over her participation in banned Tahitian dances. Two chiefs on the judicial court, Tati and Utami, hoped to increase their own influence on the court by siding with the missionaries' legal code. They warned 'Aimata that if she were brought to trial, she would lose respect in the eyes of her people. The court questioned the queen in front of the missionaries in a meeting one missionary described as "grave." 'Aimata complied with the judges' warning and agreed to stop the dances.[12]

In 1830 'Aimata again faced off with the judges. After visiting Rai'atea, the queen ordered the people on Tahiti and Mo'orea to present gifts of cloth to her and her guests from the Leeward Islands. This important ceremony, the *'a'a one*, had been conducted in every early Tahitian encounter with European visitors, and gift giving to traveling *ari'i* was customary before 1819. The missionaries encouraged Pōmare II to end the practice, due to the economic hardship it put on the Tahitian people. The missionaries intended the queen to receive proceeds from an annual tax instead.[13]

'Aimata was determined to revive the *'a'a one*. In response, four judges, including Tati and Utami, threatened to deport her. The Mamaia prophets and remaining three judges sided with the queen and charged the other four judges with rebellion. LMS missionaries also were divided on the issue. 'Aimata prepared for war. In the end the missionaries convinced 'Aimata to avoid bloodshed. 'Aimata agreed to drop her demands for cloth and, more significantly, allowed the To'ohitu judges to convict those chiefs who had honored her with the *'a'a one*.[14]

Perhaps the most momentous conflict between the queen and judges occurred over her divorce. 'Aimata had wed Tapoa, the sixteen-year-old chief of Bora Bora, in 1824 when she was nine years old. The Leeward and Windward Islands had never been united, and the betrothal was her father's strategic plan. In 1832 Tapoa led Bora Bora chiefs in an ill-advised attack against Tamatoa IV of Rai'atea. 'Aimata used Tapoa's betrayal of her Tamatoa relative as a pretext for divorce. The queen then married her cousin, Tamatoa IV's fourteen-year old grandson Tenani'a. The marriage strengthened 'Aimata's connection to the Leeward Islands.[15]

Predictably, those chiefs who opposed 'Aimata's political power used the missionaries' marriage laws as a pretext to thwart her plan. When missionary Henry Nott married 'Aimata to Tenani'a, the judges who had sided with the missionaries were forced to support the queen. Complicating these divisions was disunity among the missionaries over the queen's remarriage and the continued presence of Mamaia prophets who urged insurrectionists to resist the queen, disband the law code, and return to the old ways. This time the conflicts turned into a war in which several dozen Tahitians died before 'Aimata and her forces prevailed. Those chiefs who fought against the queen were banished from Tahiti.[16]

'Aimata had brilliantly used missionary and judicial support to publicly break the law. She strengthened her claims over both the Leeward and Windward Islands, while demonstrating that her chiefly status could not be contained by the missionaries. She gave her people reason to trust her *ari'i rahi* status. The missionaries acknowledged as much. 'Aimata's victory, they wrote, caused many Tahitians to walk away from "both law and gospel."[17]

Yet 'Aimata faced far greater political problems. Since 1767 the number of foreign visitors to Tahiti had steadily increased. By the nineteenth century, Tahiti was a pleasant stop and trading port for English merchants on their way to New Zealand and Australia, as well as for American and European whalers hunting in the Pacific Ocean. 'Aimata's grandfather and father had maximized these visits through their control of Matavai Bay and their attempts to establish monopolies over trade. In exchange, foreign vessels no longer brought nails. They brought guns, ammunition, and liquor.[18]

Port of Call

Captain Bligh of the HMS *Bounty* was the first to trade guns for food. By the early 1800s the exchange rate in Tahiti was five pigs per gun. In 1802 the HMS *Venus* ran out of pistols, gun powder, and axes before sailing away with 123,000 pounds of pork. Even the missionaries gave guns to the Tahitians. In 1807 Pōmare II wrote to LMS directors in London and thanked them for sending missionaries. He also asked for more guns and ammunition. Pōmare clearly understood the advantage of having the missionaries believe he was king of Tahiti. By 1815 Pōmare had acquired a cannon, which he installed on his canoe before sailing from Mo'orea to defeat his enemies on Tahiti.[19]

The Pōmare chiefs never were able to limit foreign trade to Matavai Bay, and the gun trade spread throughout the island. Missionary John Davies reported that Pōmare II and his supporters attended church with their guns in case anti-Pōmare clans attacked. One Sunday they did attack, and in the ensuing battle Tahitians on both sides died.[20]

'Aimata understood the importance of European trade to maintaining her power. She also believed an alliance with England's missionaries was important to maintaining her friendship with the British government, whose claims of goodwill and protection dated back to 1767. "His Majesty," Henry Canning cryptically wrote from the Foreign Office to 'Aimata in 1827, "will be happy to afford to yourself, and to your Dominions, all such Protection as His Majesty can grant to a friendly power at so remote a distance from His own Kingdom."[21]

Nevertheless 'Aimata, like her father, sought to contain the missionaries. In 1821 Pōmare II secretly forbade the chiefs on Rai'atea from selling pigs to the missionaries, in order to inflate the price missionaries paid him for food. In 1828 'Aimata attempted to channel all trade through a member of her court in a similar effort to control the prices missionaries paid for pigs and produce.[22]

But 'Aimata's greater problem lay with the foreign captains and crews who refused to obey Tahitian law. In ignoring the law and violently resist-

8. Matavai Bay, Tahiti, ca. 1820. National Library of Australia.

ing the *mutoi* (police), foreign visitors visibly demonstrated that ʻAimata was powerless to stop them. At Papeʻete drunken disorderliness and crime increased along with the sale of cheap liquor. Missionary William Ellis reported that American ships were among the worst offenders, selling rum at "an exceedingly low price." While Tahitians distilled mangoes and drank kava, the influx of foreign liquor was something different. Missionary John Orsmond noted that the "arks of the devil" brought so much rum to the island that many Tahitians could easily purchase twenty or thirty bottles each. So many Tahitians arrived drunk to church service that the missionaries dared not excommunicate anyone for fear of losing the entire church.[23]

ʻAimata and the Toʻohitu judges understood the power that foreigners wielded over the island when trading in spirits. In 1834 Tahitian judges and district chiefs met to outlaw the importation and sale of liquor. They also banned prostitution and unauthorized immigration. ʻAimata supported these legal challenges to foreign power. Still, ships smuggled liquor into the island. Ellis believed Tahiti was "verging toward complete disorganization and ruin," as a result of the foreign liquor trade, and the Tahitian court realized that foreigners would not easily submit to the penalties for lawbreaking. Ship captains and naval officers complained that their crews were not subject to Tahitian laws. They argued that missionary and merchant influence in Tahitian government constituted its own form of foreign aggression. Missionaries and merchants complicated matters by attempting to convince the chiefs that they should be *less* stringent when applying the law to foreign visitors. As Orsmond remembered, "the continual arrival of every description of ship, brought ceaseless difficulties."[24]

In the midst of these confrontations, and nearly a decade after becoming queen, 'Aimata announced to the missionaries that she was ready to become a Christian. Her announcement stunned the missionaries. In reality, by accepting Christianity 'Aimata hoped her alliance with the British Empire would be strengthened when word reached England that she had converted to its faith after years of resistance. 'Aimata wanted support from Britain in her efforts to enforce Tahitian laws over other foreign powers. In early 1836 'Aimata wrote to English missionary Henry Nott asking to join the church and participate in communion.[25]

Nott described 'Aimata's 1836 conversion and the events that preceded it as a Tahitian revival. In the *Evangelical Magazine and Missionary Chronicle*, Nott reported that beginning in late 1835, "they came in companies of ten, twenty, and thirty at a time, asking the way to Zion." While Nott later admitted he would not be surprised if some of the new Tahitian converts fell away, the missionary nevertheless believed that the general movement toward Christianity was a work of God. Missionary John Orsmond believed otherwise. "After all our talk of churches and numbers and revivals, there is not a person who comes for, or who loves Christian converse," Orsmond recalled. "The people learn the gospel as men learn military tactics."[26]

There are many reasons to accept Orsmond's view of events, as well as to doubt 'Aimata's sincerity in accepting Christianity. For example, when 'Aimata joined Nott's church in early 1836, she refused to make the required public confession of faith. Instead, the queen asked Nott for a private interview, telling him that she did not want to be embarrassed in front of her people if she did not know the answers to Nott's questions regarding the Christian faith. Nott agreed to allow 'Aimata and her husband to meet with him privately. In doing so, Nott broke LMS rules.[27]

It is likely that 'Aimata hoped to strengthen her position with Britain without betraying her Indigenous beliefs or, more likely, without allowing her people to see her submit to the foreign missionaries. Nott had already told the queen he would be leaving for England to see his Tahitian translation of the Bible printed. "But what will I say when I go to Queen Victoria?" Nott had asked 'Aimata about her lack of faith. "True," 'Aimata had replied. "I shall be ashamed for Queen Victoria to know all about [me]." From Nott's September 1835 announcement of his planned departure to his sailing for England in February 1836, the numbers of Tahitian converts to Christianity steadily increased. Nott was ecstatic when 'Aimata joined the church just two weeks before he sailed.[28]

It is also probable that 'Aimata was attempting to aid her close ally, missionary George Pritchard. Pritchard advised the queen on foreign affairs and had long been petitioning London to create a consulate in Tahiti and appoint him as British consul. Pritchard was deeply concerned by the appearance of a Catholic layman in May 1835 and feared the entrance of Catholic missionaries in Tahiti would be disastrous to the efforts of the LMS missionaries. Pritchard also was distressed by the January 1836 arrival of Jacques-Antoine Moerenhout, a Belgian Catholic and the newly appointed U.S. consul to the island. After Nott sailed for England, Pritchard renewed his request to the British foreign office to allow him to serve 'Aimata in an official capacity, and this time his request was granted.[29]

Finally, those closest to 'Aimata doubted her 1836 conversion. "She was hardly concerned with religion," her cousin and confident, Ari'ioehau, wrote after the queen's death forty years later. Only "in the last years of her life," Ari'ioehau observed, did the queen exhibit interest in Christianity and become an *etaretia* (listening member) of the Protestant church. Only after her political battles had ended did 'Aimata's interest in the church reflect nonpolitical concerns.[30]

More likely 'Aimata saw the strains of clan division and problems related to foreigners, particularly American and French sailors, as serious threats to her rule. Most likely, missionaries such as George Pritchard fed those fears with fear of their own loss of status as Protestant advisers to the crown. In turn, 'Aimata signaled through her people and family that she was willing to shift island culture toward a more formalized Protestant Christianity. Joining the Protestant church and partaking in communion was the demonstrable way she could alert LMS missionaries and their supporters in London that she was committed to their Christian cause and British nation.[31]

The French Arrive Again . . . and Again

George Pritchard had every reason to worry. In 1836 the first Catholic missionaries arrived from France, soon followed by more. In both instances the queen ordered their removal under the laws of Tahiti, which required her and the court's approval to remain on the island and forbade the teachings of Catholicism. When U.S. consul Jacques Moerenhout attempted to bring Catholic priests onto the island, an enraged Pritchard complained to the United States. In response, the United States removed Moerenhout from his position. France responded by inviting Moerenhout to serve as its consul in Tahiti. 'Aimata's decision to expel the Catholic missionaries was further complicated by several chiefs who resisted the queen's decision in order to weaken her authority over the people.[32]

These incidents began a series of events that ultimately led to French possession of Tahiti. The story is long and complicated, lasting from 1838 to 1847, and involves disaffected Tahitian chiefs, French encroachment in the Pacific, British foreign policy, Protestant missionary ambitions, and 'Aimata's attempts to maintain control of Tahiti in the midst of conflicting agendas.[33]

In 1838 French admiral Abel du Petit-Thouars traveled from Valparaiso, Chile, to investigate Tahitian treatment of French Catholic priests. French consul Moerenhout compiled a list of supposed Tahitian abuses against French nationals, including the "seizure of contraband spirits, prohibition of land sales, and conduct of the *mutoi*." At the time there were nine French nationals living on Tahiti, whose population was over 8,500. French admiral Petit-Thouars demanded that 'Aimata pay an indemnification, sign a treaty protecting French citizens, and provide a twenty-one-gun salute to his ship, the *Venus*. If she did not, the admiral warned, his ship would bombard the island. 'Aimata looked desperately to Pritchard to help raise the funds from foreign merchants living on the island. Petit-Thouars provided his own gunpowder for the salute.[34]

Next came French captain Cyrille Laplace aboard the *Artemise* in 1841. The captain demanded the abrogation of all laws against preaching or practicing the Roman Catholic faith. While Pritchard was visiting England, and 'Aimata was giving birth on the nearby island of Mo'orea, French consul Moerenhout exploited the French captain's arrival and secured the signatures of four chiefs on a written document requesting French protection. Written by Moerenhout, the letter asked the French government to send a warship to the island to help enforce Tahitian law. In Tahitian voice, Moerenhout argued that French protection was necessary "on account of the growth of evil in this land, among certain foreigners residing here, who are breaking our Laws and the Regulations of the land." Without 'Aimata's knowledge or approval, the chiefs signed the letter.[35]

'Aimata immediately denounced the document, yet in 1842 Admiral du Petit-Thouars again returned, demanding more money from 'Aimata under threat of attack. The admiral also offered the queen a way out of his continued blackmail: 'Aimata could ratify the chiefs' request by placing her signature on a document that would make Tahiti a French protectorate. Under extreme duress, 'Aimata signed the document because she could not pay the fine. In doing so, she gave France control over the island's foreign policy as well as jurisdiction over French nationals.[36]

'Aimata refused to acknowledge this forced settlement and appealed to Queen Victoria. While waiting for what she believed would be forthcoming British aid, 'Aimata flew the Tahitian flag. In response, du Petit-Thouars, who arrived for the third time in 1843, deposed the queen and annexed Tahiti. By the time King Louis-Phillipe of France denounced the admiral's actions and restored 'Aimata to her throne, hundreds of Tahitian warriors and French soldiers had died fighting each other, and French authorities had expelled Pritchard from the island. France never renounced Tahiti's status as a protectorate, however, which meant that 'Aimata was reinstated as a queen without a country, nominally ruling until her death in 1877. Her son, Pōmare V, served only three years before France formally absorbed the island. French Polynesia, in which Tahiti is its most populous island, today remains a French overseas collectivity.[37]

Sister Sovereigns

During the French-Tahitian conflict, 'Aimata wrote to Queen Victoria five times, using a secretary because she did not write Tahitian nor speak or write English. In her letters 'Aimata pleaded with Queen Victoria for England's protection against the French. 'Aimata not only based her arguments on the history of Anglo-Tahitian relations, but she also appealed to Victoria as a fellow ruler, woman, and Christian. "My Sister Queen" and "friend," she addressed the British monarch. 'Aimata admitted that the island was unable to protect itself from European powers, "to whom our institutions appear foolish, and our Government feeble," but she also chastised the English queen: "Do not to leave undone what you began, and what is so happily progressing; lend us your powerful hand; take us under your protection; let your flag cover us, and your lion defend us . . . cause our children to bless you, and to cherish your Christian feeling as we do."[38]

After fighting against domestic and foreign conflicts for nearly a decade, 'Aimata understood that her battle with France was not one she could win on her own. "Health and peace to you," she again wrote Victoria. "May you be saved by Jehovah, the foundation of our power as Queens." 'Aimata blamed the chiefs for betraying her so that "their children may govern," and she begged Victoria to send a British warship to Tahiti to enforce its protection of the island. "I am now making my last efforts. My only hope of being restored is in you," 'Aimata pleaded. "Be quick to help me, for I am like a captive pursued by a warrior, and nearly overtaken, whose spear is close to me."[39]

'Aimata also appealed to King Louis-Phillippe of France, reminding him that she, too, was a sovereign, albeit a "powerless sovereign." In defending her decision to fly the Tahitian flag against French prohibition, 'Aimata argued, "If I had complied, my Sovereign Power would have been despised by my high chiefs."[40]

'Aimata also utilized gendered arguments to gain European favor, entreating the French king to respect her womanhood. "Think of me as a woman and near giving birth to another child," she pleaded. A copy of her letter was published in the London *Times*, causing public sympathy in England to swing violently toward 'Aimata, a persuasive maneuver she and Pritchard hoped would lead to British action. In April 1846 LMS missionary Thomas Heath wrote to the Ladies Society of London on behalf of 'Aimata. He appealed to gendered sympathy and urged the Society to publish his letter on behalf of the Tahitian queen. "The names of Britain and its beloved Queen Victoria are ever on the lips of the natives," Heath told the women, "and I trust their attachment and confidence and earnest appeals will not be met by cold indifference or merely passive compassion."[41]

Throughout these public efforts 'Aimata encouraged her own people to remain calm. "Rely upon the *Justice* and the *Clemency* of the King of the French," she encouraged Tahitians in a proclamation read across the island. 'Aimata firmly believed that her people's friendship with the British government and missionaries would save their independence. "Britain will not cast us off. Let our conduct be good and wait till the letters arrive," she reminded Tahitians. In every communication, 'Aimata defended her right to rule as a birthright, just like those of the "other Sovereigns of Europe." Appealing to the laws of nations, 'Aimata stated, "I am queen of Tahiti and will stand up for my rights."[42]

There is no record that either Victoria or Louis-Philippe responded to 'Aimata during the French-Tahitian crisis of the 1840s. After 'Aimata's chiefs betrayed her, George Pritchard recorded that the queen "immediately wrote three letters, one to Louis-Philippe, one to Queen Victoria, and one to the President of the United States, disavowing all knowledge of the said document and begging that it might at once be rendered null and void." She received no reply.[43]

Victoria and Louis-Philippe did, however, discuss Tahiti with each other. In October 1844 Victoria wrote her uncle, King Leopold of Belgium, about the successful visit of Louis-Philippe to England, the first time a French king had visited an English monarch. "He spoke very openly to us all, and is determined that our affairs should go on well," Victoria reported. "He wishes Tahiti *au fond de la mer* [at the bottom of the sea]." Victoria clearly was relieved over of the king's lack of interest in the island. "The good ending of our difficulties with France is an immense blessing," she wrote Leopold, "but it is really and truly necessary that you and those at Paris should know that the danger was *imminent*."[44]

Victoria's fears were genuine. The English public had become "excited" by 'Aimata's plight, and Parliament was debating action, but Victoria adamantly wanted to avoid war with France. Other issues, too, were at stake. Most important to Victoria were the continued neutrality of the Hawaiian Islands and British colonization of New Zealand. The British government's position was clear. As long as the LMS missionaries were allowed to practice and proselytize their Protestant faith and not be physically or civilly "molested on the account of the exercise of their religion," 'Aimata and her chiefs had "acceded" to a French protectorate through their signatures.[45]

Consequently, 'Aimata's letters to Victoria went unanswered. "I am no longer called a sister because my lands have been seized," 'Aimata wrote finally to the English queen. Striking about the Tahitian crisis is that neither Victoria nor Louis-Philippe appear to have had any religious, diplomatic, or strategic interest in the island. Tahiti was an abstract problem that needed quick resolution and removal from public discourse.[46]

9. The British public sympathized with 'Aimata in her efforts to retain independence from France, as shown in this Anglophile depiction, "Queen Pomare, with her husband and children, going to church in Tahiti." *Pictorial Times*, London, 1844. National Library of Australia.

Keep Your Friends Closer

It is difficult to form an accurate picture of 'Aimata from existing source material. To the Protestant and Catholic missionaries, foreign consuls, and Euro-American naval captains, she was either intelligent or incompetent, depending on her responses to their requests. To the British and French governments, she was a nuisance. To the English public, she was tragic. 'Aimata defies a category because at one time or another she defied everyone. As Emily Manktelow reminds us, we must "untruth" the archive. In doing so a glimpse of 'Aimata emerges.[47]

As a child 'Aimata was neglected. Considered illegitimate, 'Aimata remained on Tahiti while her mother fled with the king and their supporters to Mo'orea. While Pōmare II fought his wars from abroad, 'Aimata spent "most of her time running about," attending a missionary school only intermittently. For these actions the missionaries called her "giddy and thoughtless." Initially the missionaries paid no attention to 'Aimata, occasionally noticing her in groups of young Tahitians coming to their doors for food. Later, after her ascension to the throne, the missionaries would claim that they had tried to educate her the best they could. Perhaps the strongest example of 'Aimata's neglect resides in her aloofness toward her father. As one missionary observed with surprise, 'Aimata "seemed little affected" when visiting Pōmare II's deathbed.[48]

As a young queen 'Aimata was described by various foreign sources as "sweet and good" and "pretty," yet as 'Aimata began to exercise her authority against the wishes of those foreigners, she became in their eyes "sulky and haughty." Whereas 'Aimata could be "sharp" and "cunning," to others she seemed "petulant, peevish, and capricious."[49]

To the Tahitian people 'Aimata was *ari'i rahi*. Although her position as paramount chief was constantly tested by the high chiefs, never did her people waver in their loyalty to her. Thousands of Tahitians came to hear 'Aimata in 1843 when she asked for their support against the French. "The general feeling is so far as I can find," one missionary wrote, "that they had better die than be slaves on their own land to the French." Tahitian warriors from nearly every district fought against the French in defending 'Aimata's rule. Foreigners marveled at the deference the chiefs on Rai'atea showed 'Aimata when she fled to them for protection from the French. "There is something very generous in the devotion of the chiefs and people of the Leeward Islands to her cause, even at their own risk," one observed. "There is the general idea that if she chooses to remain at Rai'atea, the sovereignty of the island will be made over to her."[50]

The Tahitian people remained loyal to 'Aimata because she was the highest chief in the islands. The fact that she was a woman was irrelevant. Nevertheless, 'Aimata's gender became a useful pawn in a complicated international game for wealth and prestige, a match played by foreigners of dubious character who were willing to lie to her to secure their privileges in the islands. Her closest advisers, missionaries George Pritchard, Alex Simpson, and John Davies, were each reported to have Tahitian mistresses, in addition to their English wives, a violation of Tahitian laws against adultery. Alex Simpson had been accused by several missionary daughters of sexual assault while serving as their teacher in a missionary boarding school. Simpson also was a "confirmed drunkard," despite the legal prohibition against spirits, and maintained a constant source of alcohol while residing at the queen's court.[51]

George Pritchard, too, used 'Aimata, involving her in numerous financial schemes, including his attempt to obtain two salaries—one as missionary and one as consul—and a currency plan that would have allowed him to flood the Tahitian market with copper coins in order to acquire the island's gold and silver. John Orsmond aptly called these fellow missionaries "whited sepulchers."[52]

Sadly, these advisers profoundly abused 'Aimata's trust. Pritchard held out to her the hope that British aid would arrive, even when he knew none was coming. On September 9, 1839, Lord Palmerston wrote to Pritchard that "Her Majesty [Queen Victoria] is bound in good faith to decline to enter any specific engagement of the kind which had been suggested." British foreign policy was clear. Due to "the great costs and difficulty" of extending British sovereignty over New Zealand, the British government would not counteract French actions in the Society Islands. "It would be dangerous and impolitic to contract similar obligations towards the inhabitants of Tahiti," the British government concluded.[53]

Pritchard, however, continued to overestimate his abilities to utilize passing English and American warships for his purposes and to counteract the same conduct of French naval officers who had acted outside the bounds of their authority. He misled 'Aimata regarding his communications with the London Foreign Office. In September 1843 the British foreign secretary Lord Aberdeen again wrote to Pritchard that the British government would not act in Tahiti. "You appear to have altogether misinterpreted" earlier instructions, Aberdeen wrote. British action, Aberdeen reiterated, would "incur the almost certainty of collision with a foreign Power." The foreign secretary added that 'Aimata had signed a treaty with France "by her own will and act," and he warned Pritchard not to suggest anything to 'Aimata that might give her false hope. "She has been ill advised to her sorrow," John Orsmond reported to LMS secretary William Ellis in London.[54]

Prichard, who the French referred to as the "daily mover and instigator" of French-Tahitian hostilities, also instilled in 'Aimata an exorbitant fear of French Catholicism. Fearing for her life, 'Aimata initially fled to a small English vessel in the harbor while she continued to wait for the

British to arrive. When they did not, she found sanctuary on Rai'atea. "I have not yet seen one proof that the French have in view to make Tahitians papists," Orsmond reported to London. In response, the missionaries accused Orsmond of siding with the French (a charge he vehemently denied), and the LMS cut ties with him. Yet Orsmond remained steadfast in his belief that 'Aimata had been needlessly caught up in an evangelical war between English Protestants and French Catholics. "It is my firm, abiding opinion that in the [French] Protectorate Pomare will be more happy, rich, powerful, honorable and safe, than all her ancestors were," Orsmond declared.[55]

Orsmond was right. In actuality, the French had no desire to manage the daily affairs of the Tahitian people. So desperate were the French to give back domestic authority to the Tahitians that they prepared to offer the government to 'Aimata's six-year-old son. Ultimately, 'Aimata's cousin Ari'ioehau traveled to Rai'atea and prevailed upon the queen to seek peace with the French and accept the protectorate. In 1847 'Aimata agreed, acknowledging that Pritchard "had not informed me fully of the contents of Lord Aberdeen's letter."[56]

When 'Aimata returned to Tahiti through Matavai Bay in 1847, the newly appointed French governor of Tahiti, Armand Bruat, welcomed the queen with great military fanfare. "The Queen was quite confused," one observer wrote. "She received the hospitality of the Governor and his wife, and was able to appreciate how much this governor, of handsome presence and of happy mood, was different from the malicious portraits that had been painted on him."[57] The French government also provided 'Aimata with a stipend of 25,000 francs per year and allowed her to retain ownership of and leases on her lands, which covered thirteen districts.[58]

Orphan Queen

Perhaps the clearest portrait of 'Aimata emerges from within her most intimate relationships. 'Aimata implicitly trusted those she believed to be her friends, such as George Pritchard. When the English government removed him from his position as consul, and the French government expelled him from the island, 'Aimata wrote, "I am now an *Orphan*." Yet even Tahitians loyal to the queen distrusted Pritchard. "Mr. Pritchard has exercised his influence fatal to the interests of the Queen," Alexander Salmon, Ari'ioehau's husband, noted.[59]

'Aimata was generous, patient, and continually surrounded by "numerous hangers on," French consul Jacques Moerenhout observed. Moerenhout called 'Aimata's retinue "*parasites*" and "*les Misérables*" but noted that the queen never complained about their presence or petitions. During the French-Tahitian War, 'Aimata risked arrest to attend the funeral of Ari'ioehau's young son, who had tragically drowned in Matavai Bay. 'Aimata "wept bitterly" when the French refused to allow her canoe to land on Tahitian soil. French sailors, watching from their ships, laughed at her tears.[60]

'Aimata also experienced personal tragedy. Her second husband, Tenani'a, was physically abusive, and 'Aimata often slept with guards outside her door. Although 'Aimata eventually would have six living children, her first three children died in infancy. "I am this year overtaken with affliction," she told a friend after the death of a daughter in 1836. "I am much troubled about my little girl."[61]

The *Pictorial Times* of London, in its attempt to support 'Aimata's cause against the French, portrayed the Tahitian queen as a delicate, white mother, clad in European attire, and attending church with her husband and sons. Yet 'Aimata was Polynesian, and foreign officials often used her motherhood against her, disparaging her for nursing her babies while listening to their demands. During *two* pregnancies, as 'Aimata lay in labor on the island of Mo'orea, Jacques Moerenhout secured important concessions from the chiefs without her knowledge and at a time when, in 'Aimata's words, "my trouble was great."[62]

Only later would the French romanticize her maternal qualities. Even then, their fictionalized depiction of 'Aimata was of a woman to be pitied. "The old woman's ungraceful bulk filled the whole breadth of her seat. She was dressed in a loose gown of crimson velvet, a stocking-less ankle was laced in slipshod fashion into a satin boot," French author Pierre Loti wrote in his 1880 novel *The Marriage of Loti*. "There still was dignity in that face, brown, wrinkled, set and hard as it was; above all else it was sad, infinitely sad."[63]

Loti's portrayal of 'Aimata was both condescending and grotesque, not unlike the depictions made by other foreigners throughout her fifty-year rule. The "good looking woman of a light olive complexion, with very dark expressive eyes and black hair," could only remain that way in the eyes of white foreigners if she projected Christian feminine submissiveness and Enlightenment virtues. Certainly raising six children to civilized adulthood, as Rousseau advocated, required 'Aimata's full attention, foreign diplomats argued. Matters of state suffered as long as they remained under 'Aimata's purview, they complained. The same men who praised 'Aimata's eyes and hair condemned her ability to combine governance and motherhood, their ridicule of the queen mitigated only when she accompanied her husband and sons to church on Sundays, dressed in satin hat and pink slippers.[64]

Conclusion

'Aimata was not immune to English and French condescensions. She understood that English missionaries viewed the Tahitians as "savages," in need of English aid, and that French statesmen belittled her as an inadequate ruler. "The poor woman is no more than the echo of the English," one French visitor observed.[65]

'Aimata was willing to echo such sentiments when it suited her purposes. "Because of your well-known benevolence," 'Aimata wrote to King Louis-Philippe, "you will not object to the petition of a Queen without power, and because of her weakness, therefore, you will compassionate her." In asking Victoria for aid, 'Aimata offered that her Tahitian people came daily into contact with "white people, superior to us in mind and body." In projecting herself as foreigners saw her, 'Aimata hoped to hold on to Tahiti's independence. Sadly, English and French policymakers simply ignored her. They could control Tahiti's destiny because 'Aimata was a powerless ally from a lesser race and inferior gender.[66]

It is right to feel anger at the ways in which 'Aimata was abused by those around her. Her inability to read or write, while appropriate for the culture into which she was born, became a permanent liability, as she relied on dubious advisers to read and translate for her. Her deft consolidation of political rule over the chiefs and missionaries was destroyed with a few strokes of a pen while she labored for her children, her pregnancies used against her. "The unfortunate 'Aimata had troubles of every sort, domestic, political, private and public," her closest friend, Ari'iehau, reflected, "until at last the missionaries, English and French, fought so violently for control of her and the island that she was fairly driven away."[67]

In appealing to the British for aid, 'Aimata petitioned the foreign power that had first approached Tahitians for its own survival. That England would not risk war with France in order to help a small island maintain its

10. *Queen Pomare*, watercolor by Jacques Antoine Moerenhout. Moerenhout was the American and French consul to Tahiti during the turbulent events of the 1840s. His watercolor exemplifies the Euro-American views of the highest chief in Tahiti. George Pritchard, *The Aggressions of the French at Tahiti and Other Islands in the Pacific.*

sovereignty is perhaps not surprising, but it is tragic nonetheless. 'Aimata's efforts to resist foreign domination were reflected in her lifelong refusal to speak or write in foreign languages or learn a Tahitian script transcribed by foreigners. These repudiations are her bequest to Indigenous political and cultural movements today. When 'Aimata died in 1877, Tahitians from every district came to Pape'ete to mourn her passing. The queen's funeral procession cut more than three miles long through the heart of the capital city.[68]

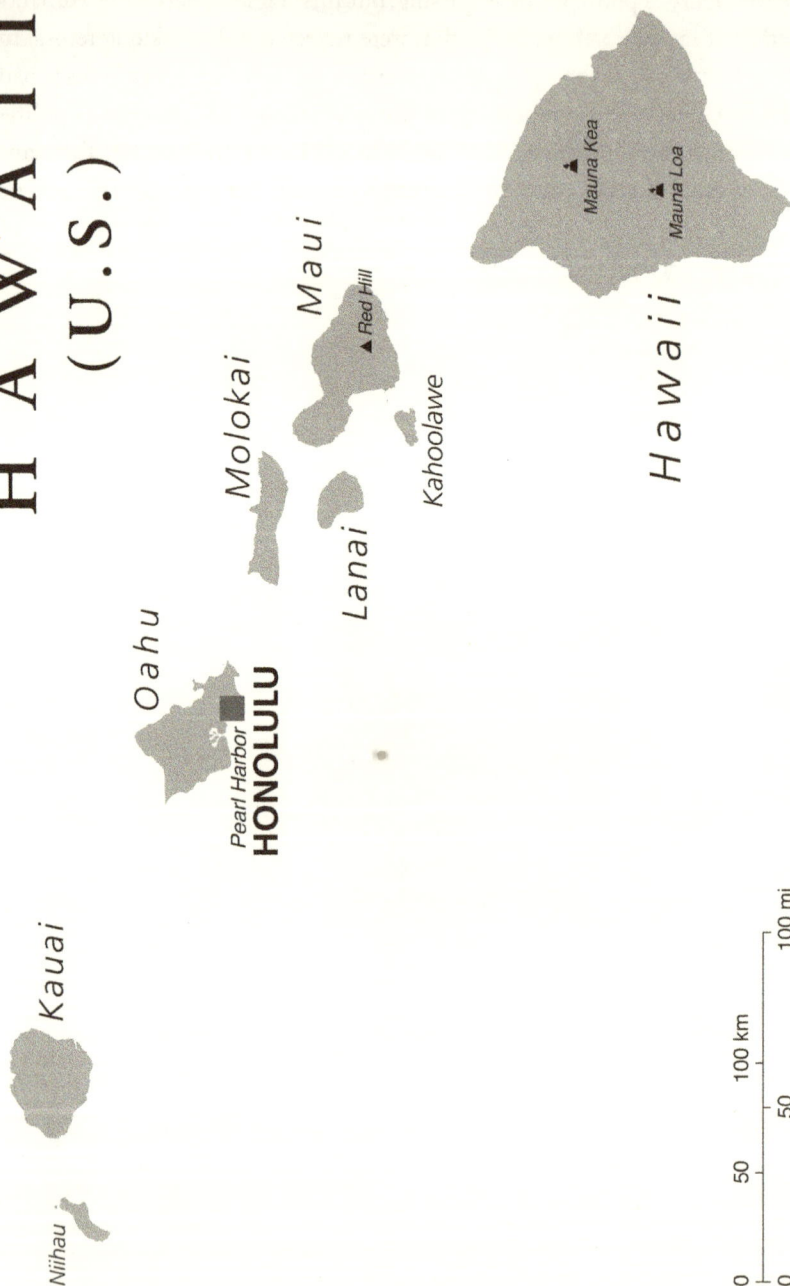

HAWAII (U.S.)

Kauai

Niihau

Oahu

Pearl Harbor
HONOLULU

Molokai

Lanai

Maui

▲ *Red Hill*

Kahoolawe

Hawaii

▲ *Mauna Kea*

▲ *Mauna Loa*

0	50		50	100 km	
0		50		100 mi	

11. Hawaiian Islands. © Peter Hermes Furian / 123RF.com.

3

❀

Ka'ahumanu

Halakau ka manu i ka lā'au.
[If it is a fine-meshed net, there is
no fish that it fails to catch.]
—HAWAIIAN PROVERB

In 1778 Captain Cook became the first white person to land in the Hawaiian Islands. When the English captain returned to the Hawaiian Islands in 1779, he arrived at an auspicious time of year during which the gods had ordained that no mortal was allowed to sail. Cook's arrival threatened the genealogically defined and deified chiefly class, who subsequently murdered Cook. Notwithstanding this event, Cook's introduction to the Hawaiian Islands opened new routes of commerce for the British, and the Royal Navy sent George Vancouver, who had been with Cook on his fatal voyage, to secure those rights. Vancouver arrived in 1792 to find that *ali'i* (chief) Kamehameha was well on his way to uniting the Hawaiian islands as their first king.[1]

Kamehameha was pleased to meet a powerful English commander with no plans of conquest but promises to protect Kamehameha's trade monopoly. Representing King George III, Vancouver returned to the Hawaiian Islands in 1794 to sign an understanding with Kamehameha. To Vancouver, British claims to the Hawaiian Islands seemed assured. Vancouver believed that Kamehameha had surrendered the Hawaiian Islands as a protectorate to Great Britain and had submitted himself and his people as "subjects of the British crown."[2]

Kamehameha viewed the alliance differently. The *ali'i* understood that Britain would send warships to aid in his conquest of rival chiefs, and he viewed Vancouver as an *ali'i* brother in his efforts to monopolize trade with

57

foreign vessels and protect his people from the "ill treatment" of foreigners, who were arriving in increasing numbers from the United States, Russia, and Spain. Kamehameha's misunderstanding of the agreement was enhanced by Vancouver's gift of materials necessary to build a warship, although the captain intended the gift only "as a protection to the royal person of Kamehameha." Vancouver's diplomatic failure of understanding would ironically aid the ascension of Hawaiian women to roles of political prominence.[3]

Island Politics

During Vancouver's first visit to the Hawaiian Islands, the English captain met a young woman who would become the most powerful woman in Hawaiian history. Ka'ahumanu was around the age of sixteen and considered by Hawaiians to be the most beautiful woman in the islands. Vancouver agreed, believing Ka'ahumanu to be "one of the finest women we had yet seen." Ka'ahumanu was the wife of Kamehameha, and they were on the cusp of becoming the most powerful *ali'i* in Hawaiian history. The captain noted that the couple appeared deeply in love. "It was pleasing to observe the kindness and fond attention, with which on all occasions they seemed to regard each other," Vancouver wrote.[4]

The partners had married in 1885 when Kamehameha was in his early twenties, and Ka'ahumanu was around the age of nine. Ka'ahumanu was infertile, and Kamehameha would marry at least twenty additional women, yet Ka'ahumanu remained his favorite wife. She was the daughter of one of Kamehameha's fiercest warriors and an *ali'i* through her own mother and father's genealogies. Described as six feet tall and handsome, Ka'ahumanu had many admirers. Nineteenth-century Hawaiian historian Samuel Kamakau was one, writing that "her arms were like the inside of a banana stalk . . . her eyes like those of a dove or the *moho* bird." Between Kamehameha's wife and his kingdom, the historian pronounced, "she was the more beautiful."[5]

Ka'ahumanu possessed what many white captains and merchants who visited the islands struggled to define. She was "proud and haughty," a "usurper of man's authority," and "born for domination," they concluded. Neither were the men from the American Board of Commissioners for Foreign Missions (ABCFM) any more generous toward Ka'ahumanu when they arrived in the islands. Ka'ahumanu was "unrestrained by a lordly husband" and had a "masculine spirit," the ABCFM missionaries complained. Only the missionary women proved insightful. "Kaahumanu has more influence in political affairs than any other person in this nation," Mercy Whitney stated.[6]

Ka'ahumanu was Kamehameha's greatest political ally. "She was valued at half his kingdom," according to Kamakau. "All her requests were granted." Ka'ahumanu accompanied Kamehameha aboard the *Discovery* to witness his alliance with Vancouver and maintained a visible partnership with her husband as he established peace in the islands after centuries of chiefly wars.[7]

By 1810 Kamehameha's military victories allowed for the couple to enact significant political reforms. They enforced new laws against murder and theft, regulated the military and economy, including the foreign trade in sandalwood, and built houses of worship to the gods. Kamehameha also appointed Ka'ahumanu to his high council, where she remained the only woman to serve in that body. On her own lands Ka'ahumanu established places of refuge where the *maka'āinana* (people) could flee for safety and plead their cases to her. "All the chiefs had the utmost confidence in her," Kamakau wrote. "Her commands were uniformly obeyed."[8]

More importantly, Ka'ahumanu exerted significant influence in preventing her family from plotting against her husband. Ka'ahumanu's brothers and cousins were prominent *ali'i* on the island of Maui, which had been forcefully conquered by Kamehameha. Kamehameha and Ka'ahumanu worked together to prevent their revolt. By dividing administration of the islands among Ka'ahumanu's family, Kamehameha kept his own relatives from obtaining political power. Ka'ahumanu gave family members generous gifts of land but required from them constant communication, further isolating her relatives from each other. "Her mind ran in the same channels as with those of the old counselors who had passed on before her," admired Kamakau.[9]

Despite the unprecedented power and unique partnership Ka'ahumanu shared with her husband, the ancient religious *kapu* (taboos) of the islands restricted the amount of authority Ka'ahumanu could exert as a woman, and Kamehameha remained a deeply religious man.[10] The true genius of Ka'ahumanu's political rule was in her ability to maintain political power after Kamehameha's death and use her power to abolish those restrictions.

Power of a Woman

As in Tahiti, the Hawaiian Islands before European contact were steeped in religious traditions that included *kapu* (taboos), which regulated all aspects

12. *Kaʻahumanu*, by Louis Choris, undated. Hawaiʻi State Archives.

of Hawaiian life. By observing *kapu* one remained in right standing with the gods, which included health and provision for the *makaʻāinana* and political power for the *aliʻi*. The *kapu* dictated times for fishing, planting, eating, leisure, worship, war, and sacrifice. *Kapu* also maintained separation among classes and between men and women. *Kahuna* (priests) presided over religious rituals and retained knowledge of the sacred genealogies that conferred *aliʻi* status. The *mōʻī* (paramount chief) enforced *kapu*. Punishments for breaking *kapu* included immediate death or death by human sacrifice. Hawaiian *aliʻi* believed that by observing *kapu*, they maintained their right to rule as direct descendants of the gods and mediators between the gods and people.[11]

Foremost among the Hawaiian gods were Kū, the god of war, and Lono, the god of fertility. Kamehameha achieved his political power through Kū because he did not possess the highest chiefly lineage in the Hawaiian Islands. He obtained *mana* through warfare. Kamehameha's wife Keōpūolani, however, held the highest status in the islands. A person who stepped on her shadow was immediately put to death. Even Kamehameha was required to strip off his clothing when in her presence. Keōpūolani's sons with Kamehameha became the heirs to his monarchy.[12]

Life in the islands was dictated by the religious calendar, which was divided into two periods, one honoring Lono and the other Kū. During the rainy season (October through February), Hawaiians rested from their agricultural labors, paid their taxes in cultivated produce to chiefs and priests, and participated in feasts and athletic games to celebrate Lono's agricultural abundance. War during this period was *kapu*. During the remaining months of the year, the war god Kū returned to preeminence, and the people began their planting season.[13]

The concept of balance was prevalent in all Hawaiian *kapu*. Those who were *kapu*, such as Keōpūolani, were considered divine. Those who were not were called *noa*. The relationship was both hierarchical and reciprocal. Consequently, one's possession of *mana*, much like in the Tahitian view, relied upon a "working fellowship." *Mana* was an active, relational concept in which chiefs and commoners played their separate roles in order to honor the gods and experience their blessing. When the chiefs and people obeyed *kapu*, they obeyed the gods and created harmony.[14]

The most stringent *kapu* regulated gender relations. In these men and women had "complementary parts to play vis-a-vis the gods," notes Caroline Ralston. Men were expected to "wrest food from divine sources," and women were to "transform the divine generative forces into children." Unlike Hawaiian men, Hawaiian women could not participate in religious sacrifices nor eat food that had been offered to the gods. Men and women were forbidden to eat together, and women were denied certain foods, such as coconut and pork. The Hawaiian taboos related to eating were known as 'aikapu.[15]

Unlike the Tahitian *tapu* system, Hawaiian *kapu* required that men cook for their families while using separate ovens for men and women. Consequently, Hawaiian families usually had two distinct eating huts for men and women and a third hut for sleeping. Hawaiian women were responsible for weaving baskets for food and mats for sleeping. They pounded bark into tapa, like their Tahitian counterparts, and fished along the shore. Hawaiian men cultivated taro and fished in the deep sea. Despite the foreign visitors who misinterpreted Hawaiian women as particularly indolent, the Hawaiian *kapu* system was more restrictive toward women than men, since the most important religious ceremonies and most sacred foods were denied to them.[16]

Kamehameha was profoundly religious. In agreeing to an alliance with Great Britain, he required Vancouver to promise that the British government would not interfere with the Hawaiian religion. When Vancouver asked Kamehameha to break a sailing *kapu* or risk losing English trade, Kamehameha reluctantly delayed the *kapu* so that he would not break it. After Vancouver left the islands, Kamehameha engaged in ritual purifying since he had dined with men he knew had dined with women.[17]

As a result of the growing number of vessels stopping in the Hawaiian Islands before making their way to Macao or the Pacific Northwest, Hawaiian *ali'i* began to declare their own *kapu* over various island products in an attempt to hoard items for trade. The *ali'i* placed *kapu* on pigs and sandalwood, profiting enormously from sandalwood extraction through the forced labor they required of their people as a form of rent for use of agricultural land. Missionary Sheldon Dibble noted that in exchange for sandalwood the *ali'i* received "guns, swords, and other instruments of death." Ultimately, Kamehameha declared all foreign trade *kapu* unless conducted by his officials on O'ahu or Maui. Sandalwood became *kapu* unless harvested for him or his designated *ali'i*.[18]

As Hawaiian *ali'i* attempted to increase their power through trade, Hawaiian women also exercised initiative in changing their cultural status. Captain Cook attempted to keep his syphilitic men from infecting Hawaiian women during his first stop in the islands. Nine months later Cook returned to find visible evidence that the disease had spread among the people. Cook's second lieutenant John Rickman explained the difficulties Cook faced in enforcing abstinence. "He soon found, that if that commerce [prostitution] was forbidden, all other trade must cease, of course, for not a pig could be purchased, unless a girl was permitted to bring it to market," Rickman wrote.[19]

Just as Purea had gifted Wallis with feathers to signify his chiefly status, Hawaiian *ali'i* consecrated Cook with their own sacred red and yellow feathers. And just as Tahitian women believed Englishmen could improve the lineage of their own genealogies, Hawaiian women hoped that bearing the child of an Englishman would raise the genealogical status of their children. Cook journaled that two to three hundred women could be found on board the *Resolution* at any given time. And just as Tahitian men prostituted their wives and daughters for material advantage, Hawaiian men realized that sexual relations with Hawaiian women could be sold to

English sailors for a price paid in iron. English sailors happily responded to all of these attentions accordingly.[20]

In meeting foreign men on board their ships, Hawaiian women also seemed unafraid to break restrictions against men and women eating together. The women were hesitant, however, to publicly break *kapu*. John Rickman wondered why women who swam out to Captain Cook's *Endeavor* at night refused to show themselves on deck during the day, not realizing that a *kapu* against entering the ocean was in place. While Hawaiian women privately ate with the sailors, they swore the crew to secrecy. Ka'ahumanu also would visit foreign ships to taste forbidden pork and shark without her husband's knowledge and despite knowing Kamehameha's penalties for breaking *kapu*. As late as 1818, Kamehameha executed Hawaiians for transgressing religious law.[21]

A Momentous Year

Despite the centuries of religious *kapu* controlled by an exclusive priesthood of men, Ka'ahumanu abolished these strictures within a matter of months. Many have attempted to explain the year 1819 in Hawaiian history. From citing cultural malaise and disenchantment with the gods to outright revolution, historians have generally pointed to religious instability as evidence that the Hawaiian pantheon no longer seemed powerful or relevant to the people and that the *maka'āinana* were ready for change. Hawaiian women who had eaten with men aboard foreign ships returned to shore alive. Hawaiian men saw Kamehameha suspend *kapu* without losing his *mana*. Meanwhile, the Hawaiian people continued to die from infectious diseases in alarming numbers, the gods seeming to have abandoned the island kingdom and those who still obeyed their laws. In 1823 native Hawaiians numbered around 135,000. Forty-five years earlier, the population had been twice the size, if not more. These explanations are compelling for their psychological insights, yet they ignore the fundamental role that Ka'ahumanu played in executing a clearly calculated plan to assume upon her husband's death the role of *mō'ī*.[22]

Before his death in 1819, Kamehameha suspected that his firstborn son through Keōpūolani might not be fit to rule. The twenty-one-year old Liholiho exhibited signs of alcoholism from the hard liquor introduced through foreign trade. Kamehameha determined that Liholiho should inherit control of the land but gave his nephew Kekuaokalani the power to enforce

13. Hawaiian women often cut their hair short and dyed it with quick lime so that it would appear white. This young woman is also wearing tapa cloth around her shoulders. "A man and woman of Sandwich Islands; Cook's Voyage *Octovo*." Library of Congress Prints and Photographs Division, LC-USZ62-24003.

kapu. Kamehameha also entrusted Kekuaokalani with his personal idol, a manifestation of the war god Kū. Dividing administrative and religious duties among different family branches was not new, but Kamehameha had demonstrated *mana* through conquest, which meant Kekuaokalani would inherit the power of war and a potential path to paramount rule.

Ka'ahumanu, her husband intended, was to serve as Liholiho's chief counselor, or *kuhina nui*, a position her father had held before his own death.[23]

What happened instead reflected Ka'ahumanu's brilliant tactical response to her husband's death on May 8, 1819. At her husband's deathbed, Ka'ahumanu gathered all of the weapons from among the *ali'i* who were present at his bedside in Kona, Hawai'i. Ten days later, after priests had consecrated Kamehameha's bones, Ka'ahumanu called for Liholiho and the *ali'i* to assemble. Surrounded by her powerful relatives who were holding muskets, Ka'ahumanu emerged, wearing a red feather cloak and yellow feather helmet and carrying Kamehameha's spear in her hand. Ka'ahumanu announced to Liholiho: "O heavenly one! I speak to you the commands of [your father]. Here are the chiefs; here are the people of your ancestors; here are your guns; here are your lands. *But we two shall share the rule* over the land."[24]

Ka'ahumanu claimed Kamehameha's sandalwood monopoly for herself and forbade Liholiho to gift away any of his father's lands. Liholiho became a "pawn" with little wealth of his own, dominated by Ka'ahumanu and her Maui relatives. As Lilikalā Kame'eleihiwa writes, "Liholiho was a weak substitute for his father, yet the *Ali'i Nui* [high chiefs] allowed him to remain as *Mō'ī* out of *aloha* [goodwill] for Kamehameha." A French visitor to the islands in August 1819 found Liholiho and his court living in virtual poverty and fishing for "the greater part of their subsistance." Captain Louis Freycinet, commanding the French *Uranie*, concurred, writing in his journal that the young king was "poorly established" and that "his wishes were frequently balked by some of the principal chiefs."[25]

Like Mother, Like Son

Ka'ahumanu would never achieve total political power under existing *kapu*, which precluded women from religious ceremonies and rituals. As long as one's *mana* resided in obedience to the *kapu* that derived from the Hawaiian gods, Ka'ahumanu's nephew held the authority through Kamehameha's war idol to challenge her rule. Consequently, Ka'ahumanu next moved to abolish the *kapu*. And like Purea, she did so in a way that demonstrated her political acumen and elevated her *ali'i* status.[26]

Ka'ahumanu used the formal installation of Liholiho as Kamehameha II to stage her rebellion and renounce *'aikapu*, the gender-based eating restrictions. At Liholiho's feast, held shortly after his father's consecration, Ka'ahumanu made her announcement: "But as for me and my people, we intend to be free from the tabus. We intend that the husband's food and the wife's food shall be cooked in the same oven, and that they shall eat out of the same calabash. We intend to eat pork and bananas and coconuts, and to live as the white people do. If you think differently, you are at liberty to do so; *but as for me and my people we are resolved to be free.*"[27]

Keōpūolani, Liholiho's mother, aided Kaʻahumanu in her rejection of *ʻaikapu*. The high *aliʻi* asked the young king if she might eat with her son Kauikeaouli, the new king's younger brother. Liholiho assented but would not join them. While periods of mourning traditionally were times of "free eating," *aliʻi* were expected to reinstate *ʻaikapu* in order to legitimize their own rule. Kaʻahumanu's investiture feast signaled to Liholiho that his *kuhina nui* planned to do more than offer advice and had no intention of helping the king go back to *ʻaikapu*.[28] Liholiho refused to follow Kaʻahumanu's family or end *ʻaikapu* that night. Instead the king returned to Kawaihae, Hawaiʻi, where he reinstituted eating restrictions, drank heavily, and nursed his grievances with his cousin Kekuaokalani. By August foreign visitors in Hawaiʻi noted that the eating *kapu* were back in full effect.[29]

Kaʻahumanu did not accept defeat. She waited while Liholiho attempted to begin his sacred duties as king. Twice Liholiho tried to consecrate a temple. Each time, Liholiho broke *kapu* due to his drunkenness. Several months later Kaʻahumanu again asked Liholiho to come to Kona and join her in abolishing *ʻaikapu*. Sensing defeat, Liholiho sailed to Kona but would not leave his canoe until Kaʻahumanu ordered her men to bring him to shore.[30]

Kaʻahumanu had prepared a feast of *kapu* foods for high-ranking men and women to eat together in violation of *ʻaikapu*. More importantly, she had prepared the feast for the night of Kukahi, the third evening of the Hawaiian lunar month and first day of Kū, the date set aside as the beginning of Makahiki, the festival of Lono. Makahiki was a ritual time established for laying down the gods before Lono. In front of everyone, Liholiho sat with Kaʻahumanu, a woman, and ate forbidden foods, demonstrating the impotency of the Hawaiian gods. Kaʻahumanu later recalled that Liholiho looked "very much perturbed."[31]

Kaʻahumanu's timing was crucial. By appropriating the ceremonies for Lono, she was able to use the Makahiki festival to abolish the Hawaiian gods. During the procession of Lono that followed the feast, chiefs and priests traditionally traveled the islands with the image of Lono and collected taxes from the people. In response, the people would offer food to the traveling *ali'i* and lay down the images of their own gods in front of Lono. In 1819 the procession took a decidedly different turn. Instead of carrying Lono's image, messengers transported the news to all districts on all islands that Liholiho had abolished *'aikapu*. Instead of temporarily laying down their wooden images in prostration before Lono, Hawaiian women *burned* them, participating with Ka'ahumanu in a *gendered* revolution that upended centuries of law and custom. By destroying the Hawaiian religion in one defiant feast, Ka'ahumanu, like Purea, demonstrated that gender had no place in governance. By forcing Liholiho to accept her demands, she showed the *ali'i* and *maka'āinana* that she was, in fact, the paramount ruler.[32]

Not all welcomed Ka'ahumanu's revolution. The priests, as well as many chiefs and commoners, were outraged. In December 1819 Kamehameha's nephew Kekuaokalani formed an army to invade Maui and assert his *mana* over Ka'ahumanu and her family. Ka'ahumanu, leading a squadron of canoes, met him near Kuamo'o, Maui. Ka'ahumanu's forces possessed nine hundred muskets that Ka'ahumanu had purchased from foreigners, a swivel gun mounted on a canoe, and more ammunition than her enemies. Her warriors defeated Kekuaokalani, killing him and his wife Manono in the battle. Ka'ahumanu had defeated the *ali'i* charged with protecting *kapu*. She had won a war during a *kapu* month for war. She was victorious over the war god Kū and now could banish him and all of the Hawaiian gods permanently.[33]

Path to Salvation

Three months after Ka'ahumanu's amazing victory, the first American missionaries arrived. Ka'ahumanu was away when the missionaries anchored off the coast of Maui. The twenty-two missionaries, including fourteen men and women, five children, and three returning Hawaiian converts, had been at sea for six months and were seeking permission from Liholiho to land. Liholiho did not respond. The king was waiting for Ka'ahumanu. The *Missionary Herald* would later report to its American readers that the Hawaiian chiefs "pretended to be waiting" before allowing the missionaries ashore. It took time for the missionaries to realize that a woman held absolute power in the islands.[34]

Ka'ahumanu had not replaced the Hawaiian gods with any other gods, and when the missionaries heard about the religious revolution which had taken place, they believed that they had arrived at an "auspicious moment" in God's providential history. Over the next several years, the missionaries worked tirelessly to learn the Hawaiian language, transcribe it into written form, and translate the Bible for the Hawaiian people. They preached, built homes, and set up a printing press. The missionaries intended to stay.[35]

Ka'ahumanu, by contrast, was a uniquely secular woman. After abolishing the religious *kapu*, she raised a pet pig, an animal once forbidden to pen, eat, or touch. Ka'ahumanu initially was uninterested in the missionaries, but, like 'Aimata in Tahiti, she was faced with domestic and foreign conflicts whose escalation threatened her rule. These events influenced her growing relationship with the missionaries. Her decision to be baptized into Christianity and declare laws based upon the Bible were directly linked to her fear that foreign governments would seek to rule her nation.[36]

Ka'ahumanu already was familiar with Christianity. George Vancouver had attempted to convert her husband and had offered to send missionaries from England. Ka'ahumanu realized that the European ships who visited the islands represented nations who shared the same god, but Ka'ahumanu also understood that relations among those nations were complex. Some *ali'i* feared Americans would attempt to deceive the Hawaiian people into believing they were English and take advantage of the British-Hawaiian alliance. When the French *Uranie* arrived, Ka'ahumanu queried Captain Freycinet about rumors that the French were planning to steal the islands as well.[37]

Ka'ahumanu had reason to worry. Her cousins Kālaimoku and Boki were strategizing against her. They sought the company of Liholiho's French interpreter, Jean Rives, and received Catholic baptism on board the *Uranie*. Liholiho also attempted to reassert power, taking as one of his wives Kekaiha'akulou, wife of Kaumuali'i, the prominent *ali'i* of Kaua'i. Kaumuali'i paid tribute to Ka'ahumanu, and by sharing a wife with him, Liholiho hoped to divert tribute away from Ka'ahumanu and toward himself. Ka'ahumanu deflected Liholiho's maneuver in dramatic fashion. She married Kaumuali'i and kept his tribute.[38]

These internal contests for political power threatened to extend into international affairs. In desperation Liholiho sailed for England in November 1823. He was an impoverished puppet king, and he hoped King George, as an *ali'i* brother and fellow *mō'ī*, would honor the diplomatic alliance with his father and help Liholiho assert his authority over Ka'ahumanu. Ka'ahumanu countered by approaching the American missionaries for Christian baptism.[39]

It is telling that the American missionaries initially denied Ka'ahumanu's request for baptism. Like 'Aimata, Ka'ahumanu had complex reasons for seeking to adopt the missionaries' faith. Sensing perhaps that Ka'ahumanu's motivations were not entirely religious, the missionaries told her to wait. They wanted to see if Ka'ahumanu demonstrated true Christian conversion.[40]

Likely Ka'ahumanu was concerned about the political ramifications of Liholiho's departure for England and the response King George might give to Liholiho's request for British aid. By accepting the "white man's god," Ka'ahumanu demonstrated to the English, Americans, and French that she, unlike Liholiho, was willing to rule her nation in the same manner as their own rulers. Missionary William Richards observed, "[Ka'ahumanu] prefers to go before, rather than follow others, and consequently, whenever she acts, she acts in such a manner to distinguish herself from others."[41]

Ka'ahumanu actively began to court the missionaries, asking them to teach her to read and write. Other foreigners had refused to teach ali'i the palapala (written word), believing such knowledge would interfere with their own agendas. Ka'ahumanu appreciated that the American missionaries were different. One of the first sentences Ka'ahumanu wrote in her own hand suggests her rationale for accepting missionary influence: "I am making myself strong."[42]

Ka'ahumanu also invited the missionaries to influence Hawaiian law. On Maui Ka'ahumanu outlawed drunkenness and mandated Sabbath worship and education for all residents. Declaring the new kapu around the island, Ka'ahumanu's messengers must have seemed to the Hawaiian people like the priests of Lono announcing a new season. Samuel Kamakau believed that Ka'ahumanu adopted the new religion to "improve the condition of the government" and "build a greater nation." Certainly, Ka'ahumanu hoped that missionary schools and compulsory education would strengthen her people's ability to reject foreign manipulations.[43]

In March 1825 Ka'ahumanu received word that Liholiho and his wife Kamāmalu had died in London of measles. Ka'ahumanu's cousin Boki brought the bodies back to Honolulu. He also brought stories of a nation in which those who possessed the palapala held great dominion over those who did not. Unfortunately for Boki, King George IV had told the delegation he would not interfere in Hawaiian politics. Vancouver's alliance with Kamehameha did not extend to his son nor past the limits of English trade. Encouraged by the news, Ka'ahumanu continued her efforts to build schools and began her governance over eleven-year-old Kauikeaouli (Kamehameha III). On December 4, 1825, nearly two years after her initial request, the missionaries baptized Kaʻahumanu into the Christian faith.[44]

Visitors

Even before the first American missionaries arrived in 1820, Hawaiian *aliʻi* knew that Tahitians possessed the *palapala*. Hawaiian chiefs were concerned by this strategic advantage. When LMS missionary William Ellis sailed from Tahiti to Honolulu in 1822, Kaʻahumanu feared a political crisis. Ellis intended to visit the ABCFM missionaries, and he brought with him five Christian Tahitians, including, the "tall and commanding" Auna, a former *ʻarioi* warrior who had fought with Pōmare II in his successful battle to unite Tahiti.[45]

Kaʻahumanu and her council immediately met with the group. She then asked to speak with Auna alone. The questions on Kaʻahumanu's mind were political, not religious. Did the group's arrival signal that Pōmare II had hostile intentions toward the Hawaiian Islands? Were the English missionaries a dangerous threat to the Tahitian people? Auna responded negatively to both questions, assuring Kaʻahumanu that Pōmare had no intention of invading the Hawaiian Islands. Auna also promised Kaʻahumanu that the Tahitians would not use their connections with the American missionary population against her. Kaʻahumanu allowed the small group to stay.[46]

The American missionaries welcomed William Ellis as a white, Polynesian-speaking Christian who could help them translate the Bible into the Hawaiian language. Liholiho hoped Ellis, an Englishman, would accompany him to London to translate his grievances against Kaʻahumanu to King George. Keōpūolani, however, welcomed the Tahitians as family and became the first Hawaiian to convert to Christianity. Just as they had introduced the *ʻaikapu* hundreds of years before, Tahitians again influenced the religious trajectory of the islands. With Keōpūolani's conversion, other *aliʻi* began to follow. Three years before Kaʻahumanu's own baptism, Keōpūolani had, once again, used her *mana*, the highest in the islands, to help Kaʻahumanu establish a new religious order. For native historian Samuel Kamakau, the actions of both women were the "long *malo* [cloth] uniting the kingdom from Kahiki [Tahiti] to Hawaii."[47]

Even after the missionaries accepted Kaʻahumanu into their church, the *kuhina nui* faced challenges to her political authority. Her greatest resistance

14. *Ka'ahumanu,* pen, ink wash, and watercolor by Louis Choris, 1816.
Honolulu Museum of Art. The Picture Art Collection / Alamy Stock Photo.

came from the increasing number of American and British sailors who were
arriving in the islands and violating Hawaiian laws. To protect Hawaiian
women from being abused, bought, and even kidnapped by foreign men,
Ka'ahumanu placed a *kapu* on prostitution. The international response was
staggering. Diplomats protested, sailors rioted, and captains allied with
Ka'ahumanu's cousin Boki, who provided their crews with access to an
illegal sex trade. Ka'ahumanu, in an effort to contain Boki, used *kapu* laws

prohibiting adultery and drunkenness against him. In retaliation, Boki plotted to assassinate her. So significant were the conflicts over Ka'ahumanu's laws against prostitution that the uss *Dolphin* and British whaling vessel *John Palmer* bombed the Honolulu shoreline in 1826 and 1827 to protest the prostitution ban. In both instances Ka'ahumanu was forced to temporarily lift her *kapu* against the sex trade.[48]

These serious acts of foreign defiance would increase throughout the nineteenth century and eventually lead to the loss of Hawaiian sovereignty. Nevertheless, during her lifetime Ka'ahumanu retained her political position, the loyalty of most *ali'i*, and the respect of the Hawaiian people. As Kamakau recorded, "There was no one equal to fill her place."[49]

Legacies of Law

Traveling around the islands with Ka'ahumanu, the Tahitian warrior Auna marveled at the "multitudes" of people who met her with gifts of poi, hogs, dogs, bananas, and tapa. Auna understood that these were items of value reserved for the highest *ari'i*. His own Tahitian kingdom was several years away from experiencing a woman's paramount rule. Hawaiians also brought their idols to Ka'ahumanu so that she could witness their obedience in destroying the idols and their willingness to follow her leadership despite the social upheaval caused by her political manueverings.[50]

Ka'ahumanu, like 'Aimata in Tahiti, came to believe that an alliance with the Christian missionaries was her best path forward in a globalizing Pacific world. Ka'ahumanu's relationship with the missionaries evolved along with her political realities, impacting not only Hawaiians but the missionaries themselves. American missionary wives had not planned to be active in their husbands' evangelizing efforts. In fact, the ABCFM was quite clear that a woman's role was inside the missionary home. Nevertheless, the practicalities of Ka'ahumanu's power and her particular interest in the missionary women led to their increased role in teaching Hawaiians to read and write, as well as the missionaries' greater emphasis on offering Hawaiian women the *palapala*. The conversion of influential women such as Keōpūolani and Ka'ahumanu also signaled a significant success to ABCFM supporters back in the United States, as accounts of Polynesian female nakedness and sexuality were, in fact, among the original impetus for the Protestant missionary movement.[51]

15. Missionary Hiram Bingham and Kaʻahumanu travel the
islands to preach Christianity. "N-1348—Kaahumanu:
'The Queen at Waimea, Oahu recommending Christianity.'
Photograph." Mission Houses Museum Library.

In strengthening her own rule, Kaʻahumanu elevated the role of American
women living the islands. Kaʻahumanu spent much time with the missionary women, and when missionary men finally realized Kaʻahumanu's true
political power, her relationship with their wives had become the primary
avenue for introducing Christianity to the Hawaiian people. The irony of
these events is that nearly a century later American missionary women were
still coming to the islands. But these progressive feminists seemed to know
nothing of Kaʻahumanu's earlier political revolution. Several generations
of American missionaries had successfully consolidated Hawaiian political
culture into one resembling their own.[52]

Kaʻahumanu's efforts to secure the cultural freedom and political power
of women did not end at her death in 1832. Kīnaʻu and Kekāuluohi, also
wives of Kamehameha, both followed Kaʻahumanu as *kuhina nui* to Kamehameha III, using their premierships to continue her agenda.[53]

Kaʻahumanu ultimately increased her political authority by weaken-
ing the power of her wards, Kamehameha II and III. American advisers
to Kamehameha III and his successors would weaken the power of the
Hawaiian monarchy entirely. They did so by creating a legislature. Over

time, the Hawaiian legislature would adopt governance that reflected the birth country of its American advisers, banning women's suffrage as well as the rights of women to serve in the legislature. Nevertheless, their first constitution praised Ka'ahumanu by name: "It shall be the duty of the King to appoint some chief of rank and ability, to be his particular minister, whose title shall be Premier [*Kuhina Nui*] of the Kingdom. His office and business *shall be the same as that of Kaahumanu.*... For even in the time of Kamehameha I, life and death, condemnation and acquittal were *in the hands of Kaahumanu.*"[54] It certainly seems as if the political authority of a woman was accepted and praised within the Hawaiian kingdom into the middle of the nineteenth century.

Conclusion

Foreign statesmen failed to understand the esteem Ka'ahumanu held in the eyes of the Hawaiian people. Just as they ridiculed 'Aimata, who refused to speak their language and mothered her children in front of them, white visitors to the Hawaiian islands refused to admire Ka'ahumanu. Unfortunately, one reason was because of her size. Hawaiian *ali'i* women were large. Visitors often guessed three hundred pounds, although those estimates most likely were high. Rose de Freycinet wrote in her journal, "Imagine a woman in her thirties, 5 feet 10 inches tall, fat not in proportion to her height, but out of all proportion—in short, enormous." Rose's husband, French captain Louis de Freycinet, was even less generous: "These female colossi, who seemed to exist only to eat and sleep, looked upon us mostly with a stupid air." Freycinet was much annoyed when his audience with Liholiho could not begin until Ka'ahumanu arrived.[55]

Like Tahitian women who undertook special diets to gain weight, Hawaiian *ali'i* women spent their young adulthoods tightly wrapping themselves in tapa while eating poi to achieve their society's standards of beauty. Modern women and men apply the same rigor to diet and appearance, albeit to achieve the opposite effect. Where Americans and Europeans saw laziness, indolence, and selfishness, Hawaiian women saw spiritual blessing, provision, and rest, a reminder that cultures can be delicate and easily damaged by condescension and condemnation.[56]

Of course, what eroticized French writers and disgusted English and American missionaries were Polynesian standards of (un)dress. Most foreigners did not appreciate the labor-intensive process of pounding bark

16. Kaʻahumanu with servant. "N-1366—Kaahumanu: engraving by Choris. Photograph." Mission Houses Museum Library.

into cloth or using nature to produce color. For Hawaiians, creating tapa was women's work because cultivating taro was not. In these gendered divisions of labor, many Hawaiians saw spirituality.[57]

Kaʻahumanu did not. She rejected the gendered divisions of labor as defined by the Hawaiian gods and instead embraced the missionaries' god, not realizing the full implication of Protestant gender strictures. Kaʻahumanu's decisions followed the same countercultural path she and Keōpūolani had taken when they first broke ʻaikapu, yet Hawaiian women and law would grapple with American standards of domesticity and labor for the remainder of the century.

4

Lili'uokalani

E ma uke ea o ka 'āina. Ma kou pono mau.
A ma kou mana nui. E ola e ola ka mō'ī.
[Grant your peace throughout the land. Over
these sunny isles, keep the nation's life, oh
Lord, and upon our sovereign smile.]
—LILI'UOKALANI
("Song of the Hawaiian Nation," 1866)

Ka'ahumanu was not a queen in the English sense of the word, yet she possessed more power than her English counterpart, Victoria. 'Aimata, who ruled as an European-styled queen, came to the throne nearly a decade before the British monarch. Hawaiian queen Lili'uokalani would travel to London to meet her "sister sovereign" during Victoria's Golden Jubilee. All four women believed they rightly held political power and presided over sovereign nations.

In 1891 Hawaiian *ali'i* Lili'u Loloku Walania Kamaka'eha, known as Lili'uokalani, became the first sovereign queen and last monarch of the Hawaiian Kingdom. She was fifty-two years old. After a two-year reign, the Christian ruler was overthrown by white businessmen and landowners, many of whom were the sons and grandsons of American missionaries. The concerns of these men, who called themselves the "Hawaiian League," were rooted in their history, one in which a decline in the native population persisted, the number of foreign residents grew, and the American missionaries' influence on Hawaiian law and culture continued. All of these conditions favored the political and economic aspirations of the *haole*,[1] until Lili'uokalani attempted to make changes to the white political order.

When Ka'ahumanu sided with the American missionaries in the 1820s, she did so in the belief that she was equipping her nation to regulate the actions of foreigners visiting her islands. Kauikeaouli, Alexander Liholiho, and Lota Kapuāiwa (Kamehameha III, IV, and V), to varying degrees, accepted Ka'ahumanu's foreign policy and continued to seek the advice of American and European advisers. Yet the problems their Hawaiian subjects faced grew.[2]

During the 1840s some American missionaries quit their positions with the ABCFM to serve in the Hawaiian government. Men such as Gerrit Judd and William Richards urged the king to increase agricultural productivity by giving Hawaiians individual titles to the land on which they communally subsisted. These efforts were made in conjunction with legal changes regarding the family. Both initiatives reflected American Protestant values regarding labor and gender.[3]

Christian missionaries had encouraged Ka'ahumanu to outlaw adultery and fornication. To encourage Hawaiians to live as nuclear families rather than in kinship groups or *hānai* (foster) relationships, the missionaries promoted coverture laws in which a husband legally controlled his wife's assets and held custody of their children. The husband assumed his wife's property and debts upon and during marriage. A married woman was considered, according to the 1845 Hawaiian marriage contract laws, "civilly dead."[4]

Missionaries believed that forcing Hawaiian fathers to grow cash crops and mothers to raise children in the home would end the horrible population decline that they attributed to indolence and alcohol. They were correct that the population was in decline. By the 1850s the native population in the islands had decreased 75 percent, largely due to the physical and psychological effects of foreign diseases such as smallpox, influenza, and syphilis. Lili'uokalani's sister Kaimina'auao, for example, died of measles at the age of three.[5]

Changes to marital law coincided with the Māhele, an unprecedented series of laws between 1848 and 1850 in which Kamehameha III divided crown lands between the people, chiefs, and government. All heads of households, including foreigners, could receive title to the lands they occupied or purchased through fee simple. While many Hawaiians gained deeds to their land, additional laws ended common grazing rights in the uplands and required landowners to pay their property taxes in hard currency. As one missionary noted: "The soil is good, but it is not adapted for the cultivation of silver and gold. Consequently, all our able-bodied men have gone money hunting."[6]

Kamehameha III and other *ali'i* realized that industrialization required capital. Western symbols of wealth and long-term survival in an economy heavily influenced by foreign residents necessitated that the government demand taxes in something other than taro and pigs. Due to the increase in taxes on the native population, the Māhele produced the opposite result of its intended purpose. It placed large tracts of land into the hands of those who owned capital, the foreign residents. By the 1890s Hawaiians possessed only 14 percent of all taxable land but represented over 60 percent of the population.[7]

Some Hawaiian women gained influence during the Māhele as they occupied land for their husbands and sons who emigrated to urban areas in search of paid employment. Many landholders also were widows who had lost their husbands to successive disease outbreaks in the 1850s. Nevertheless, the intent of government advisers was to transform native cultural practice into a replica of American labor history. The Protestant missionaries attached theology to their views of gendered labor. As one ABCFM missionary instructed, "It is the husband's role to work out-doors—he farms and builds the home and prepares that which concerns the welfare of the body." The role of the wife, missionaries taught, "is to maintain the house and all that is within." In her study of missionary wives, Patricia Grimshaw notes, "The teaching of submissiveness, then, was intimately related to the encouragement of women to lead a domestic-oriented existence based on gender division of labor in the American mode."[8]

Asked to reject hundreds of years of culture built on the subsistence farming of taro, communal use of lands, kinship networks of parenting, and gendered divisions of labor that did not reflect missionary ideals of womanly domesticity, the native population became prey to sugar planters. Ka'ahumanu's efforts on behalf of Hawaiian women had become entangled with the ramifications of her alliance with the missionaries.[9]

Woman in Office

In 1840 King Kamehameha III instituted the Hawaiian kingdom's first constitution, which outlined the important role Ka'ahumanu had held as *kuhina nui*. The king also appointed four *ali'i* women to the newly created

17. Liliʻuokalani, ca. 1853. Queen Liliuokalani Photograph
Exhibition. Hawaiʻi State Archives.

House of Nobles. The political rights held by Hawaiian women declined
the remainder of the nineteenth century. In 1850 Hawaiian law formally
denied women the right to vote, and by 1854 they no longer sat in the lower
house of the legislature. Alexander Liholiho (Kamehameha IV) appointed
the last *aliʻi* woman to the House of Nobles in 1855. The 1864 constitution
eliminated the position of *kuhina nui*.[10]

Instead Kamehameha III created a legislative process by which his authority would be tested by non-Hawaiians who now owned land and participated
in government. Watching the continued diminution of Hawaiian women's

political power, young Lili'uokalani understood that these political changes were encouraged by foreigners for their "personal benefit."[11]

When Alexander Liholiho became Kamehameha IV in 1854, he attempted to shift the monarchy away from American influence. Liholiho and his wife Emma invited an English Anglican bishop to serve the kingdom and hoped to keep the constitutional monarchy patterned after Great Britain. Liholiho and Emma also planned to send their young son to England for his education, in order to "get him as far as possible out of the educational range of New England missionaries." Their efforts slowed but did not stop American influence or the Hawaiian legislature's power.[12]

By the second half of the nineteenth century, Hawaiian monarchs were struggling in their efforts for continued independence as kings of a sovereign state. Their long-standing relationship with Great Britain was an important counterweight to the interests of white sugar planters in the islands who wanted the monarchy to pursue trade reciprocity with the United States. Many of the most successful landowners were the descendants of ABCFM missionaries who had benefited from the Māhele. In return for reciprocity, the United States wanted Pearl Harbor. David Kalākaua, who came to the throne in 1874, secured treaties with the United States for trade reciprocity and the sole use of Pearl Harbor. Tax revenue to the Hawaiian government increased, but Kalākaua attempted to distance himself from the missionary descendants by joining the Anglican church, appointing a Mormon (Walter Murray Gibson) as his foreign minister, reviving the ancient hula dances, and reinstituting traditional *kahuna* priests.[13]

Kalākaua's actions created unrest among the *haole* class. In 1887 the Hawaiian League forced Kalākaua to sign a new constitution, arguing that Kalākaua's efforts to license opium had created too much government corruption. The new constitution eliminated the king's ability to appoint members to the House of Nobles. It also required a member of the king's cabinet to cosign all of the king's actions. A cabinet of men now held the power that Ka'ahumanu once had over the Hawaiian king. Kalākaua could not remove a cabinet minister without a majority vote of the legislature.[14]

Lili'uokalani observed these actions against her brother with dismay. Viewing the "Bayonet Constitution" very differently than the Hawaiian League, Lili'uokalani wrote, "As [the American residents] became wealthy . . . their greed and their love of power proportionately increased." Lili'uokalani nicknamed the Hawaiian League the "Missionary Party" in reflection of its members' genealogical histories. She believed they were secretly plotting to overthrow the king.[15]

No coup was necessary. Kalākaua died unexpectedly just two years after signing the Bayonet Constitution, and Liliʻuokalani ascended to the throne in 1891. Her right to rule was based on the Hawaiian kingdom's long history of chiefly genealogies but also upon the Hawaiian constitution, which allowed a king to appoint his successor.[16]

Liliʻuokalani ruled only two years before she was overthrown by the Hawaiian League, which then established a white republic. In her efforts as queen, Liliʻuokalani attempted to institute a new constitution in which non-naturalized foreigners would be disenfranchised, the monarchy would regain the ability to appoint members to the House of Nobles, and the queen could remove her own cabinet members without the consent of the legislature. For her efforts to increase the power of native Hawaiians and strengthen the monarchy, Liliʻuokalani lost the kingdom.[17]

A Good, Good Christian Woman

As a politician Liliʻuokalani led her cabinet with Christian humility. One biographer noted that she may have been *too* Christian.[18] Educated by the missionaries, Liliʻuokalani had accepted Christianity and the rule of law. By seeking signatories from her cabinet for the new constitution, as required by the Bayonet Constitution, Liliʻuokalani displayed her honest intentions, yet she was betrayed at every turn by those she considered her Christian brothers. Her cabinet rebelled. "They could not be satisfied even with the splendid results which our continued nationality offered them," Liliʻuokalani wrote. "They became fiercely jealous of every measure which promised to benefit the native people."[19]

Of the thirteen members of the Committee of Public Safety that organized the 1893 revolution, three were missionary descendants, four were Americans, and the rest were naturalized and non-naturalized white foreigners. None was native Hawaiian. Additionally, Sanford Ballard Dole, son of ABCFM missionaries, became the de facto leader of the movement and the first president of the Hawaiian Republic. "I never saw a more unchristian like set as these Missionaries," Liliʻuokalani wrote in her diary three weeks after the revolution. She called the new provisional government the "Missionary P.G.," so closely did she align the revolutionaries with the American missionaries and their heirs.[20]

Lili'uokalani also may have been too *Hawaiian* in her cultural approach to these events. Lili'uokalani believed in the ancient art of negotiation. When warfare among chiefs became too deadly, Hawaiian *ali'i* paused, laid down their arms, and attempted to secure agreement between conflicting sides. When members of her own cabinet leaked the contents of the constitution to the Committee of Public Safety and then refused to sign the document after leading Lili'uokalani to believe they would, the queen mistook their refusal as the beginning of negotiations. Instead, over the next forty-eight hours the Committee of Public Safety formed a provisional government, drafted a treaty of U.S. annexation, and asked American consul John Stevens to bring ashore U.S. marines on board the uss *Boston*, in order to protect American lives and property from "royal aggression."[21]

When 162 marines landed in Honolulu on Monday, January 16, Lili'uokalani asked Stevens to remove them. While the queen waited for a response from Stevens, the committee and their supporters occupied 'Iolani Palace and established a new government. The entire revolution was over by the evening of January 17, 1893.[22]

The provisional government immediately sought U.S. annexation and permanent trade reciprocity. It also expelled the queen from 'Iolani Palace and confiscated all government lands, including the queen's personal holdings. Lili'uokalani, in response, yielded her authority, not to the provisional government, but to the United States, hoping that the Christian nation would recognize the injustice of the revolution. In her surrender Lili'uokalani explained her rationale: "To avoid any collision of armed forces, and perhaps the loss of life, I do, under this protest and impelled by said forces, yield my authority until such time as the government of the United States shall, upon the facts being presented to it, undo the action of its representative, and reinstate me in the authority which I claim as the constitutional sovereign of the Hawaiian Islands."[23] In surrendering to the U.S. government, Lili'uokalani signaled that she believed her nation to be equal to the United States and her political authority to be the same as the U.S. president.

To his credit, newly inaugurated President Grover Cleveland removed the annexation treaty from Congress. The treaty had been forwarded to the U.S. Senate by outgoing president Benjamin Harrison in early 1893 immediately following the revolution. Cleveland ordered an investigation of the Hawaiian Revolution and appointed James Blount to travel to the islands to investigate what had happened. In a 1,400-page report, Blount sided with Lili'uokalani. When President Cleveland asked Lili'uokalani to spare the lives of the revolutionaries, she agreed. When Cleveland asked the provisional government to restore the monarchy, it refused. President Dole replied to the United States in striking language: "We do not recognize the right of the President of the United States to interfere in our domestic affairs. Such right could be conferred upon him by the act of this government . . . or it could be acquired by conquest. This I understand to be the American doctrine." Dole, too, believed the Hawaiian republic to be equal to the United States.[24]

President Cleveland referred the matter to Congress. "I believe that a candid and thorough examination of the facts will force the conviction that the provisional government owes its existence to an armed invasion by the United States," the president wrote. "We should endeavor to repair a substantial wrong." Although the House of Representatives censured Stevens, Congress declined to go to war against the white descendants of Americans living in the islands. The Republican Party added the pursuit of Hawaiian annexation to its party platform.[25]

In 1895 a small group of Hawaiian loyalists attempted to restore Lili'uokalani's monarchy through force of arms. One bystander was killed. The Hawaiian government charged Lili'uokalani with treason. In order to spare the lives of those loyalists arrested in the attempted coup, Lili'uokalani formally abdicated her throne, ending the Hawaiian monarchy. Tried by a military tribunal of men, she was declared guilty of misprision and sentenced to eight months imprisonment, five years hard labor (not carried out), and two years parole, during which time she was not to attend church or meet with any groups of people.[26]

In her statement to the court, Lili'uokalani included a strong defense of the Hawaiian people, who had been accused of plotting violence against *haole* women and children, a gendered and slanderous attack meant to appeal to any *haole* who may have been wavering in their commitment to try the queen. Lili'uokalani responded: "It would have been sad indeed if the doctrine of the Christian missionary fathers, taught to my people by them and those who succeeded them, should have fallen like the seed in the parable upon barren ground," the queen stated. "I assure you, who believe you are faithfully fulfilling a public duty, that I shall never harbor any resentment or cherish any ill feeling toward you, whatever may be your decision."[27]

Lili'uokalani argued that religious bonds superseded racial and gender differences. She was a "good, good Christian woman," her *hānai* daughter Lydia Aholo explained. Lili'uokalani's attempts to play by American political rules were not enough for those who viewed her native queenship as detrimental to their continued white privileges in the islands.[28]

Lili'uokalani's charitable feelings toward those who supported the revolution were further tested in 1898. During the Spanish American War, President William McKinley asked Congress to secure the perpetual use of Pearl Harbor through annexing the Hawaiian Islands. The joint resolution passed the House of Representatives 209 to 91 and the Senate 42 to 21. The new governor of the Territory of Hawaii, Sanford Ballard Dole, raised the United States flag on August 12, 1898, over Iolani Palace, the queen's former home.[29]

Mrs. Dominis

In their arguments against the queen, Lili'uokalani's political enemies placed her race, gender, and sexuality on trial before the white world. During the revolution, ABCFM missionary Sereno Bishop sent scathing letters to the American press, calling the queen's influence "debauching" and "perverting." Under the name "Kamehameha," Bishop anonymously wrote columns for the *Washington (DC) Evening Star*, describing the queen as "treacherous," "despotic," and "sensual." Lili'uokalani was a "Polynesian woman," Bishop warned, which meant that she had inherited "deviances" that white women had not. Newspapers published rumors that Lili'uokalani had taken a Tahitian lover after the death of her white husband. They repeated gossip that her husband had been unhappily married and sexually unsatisfied. They accused the queen of shedding "crocodile tears" for Christian morality, while secretly "aroused" by her "lust" for power. The sexualized language was meant to shock readers into viewing the queen as a deviant woman, doubly incapable of rule.[30]

Arguing for the prosecution at Lili'uokalani's trial, *haole* attorney William Kinney reminded the tribunal that "much that is in her statement" could be "passed by" because Lili'uokalani was a woman. In her diary Lili'uokalani noted the constant "animosity" that followed her "not only as a queen, but as a woman," and marked the numerous times she was referred to as "that woman" or her movements described as "haughty" and "arrogant." Lili'uokalani also believed that if her *haole* husband John Dominis had been alive,

18. Queen Liliʻuokalani in 1900. Queen Liliuokalani
Photograph Exhibition. Hawaiʻi State Archives.

"they would never have dethroned [me]." Sanford Dole confirmed as much in his own memoirs, noting that with the death of Dominis, the queen lost "a level-headed advisor," a white man who would check her native, feminine impulses.[31]

It is likely that Liliʻuokalani's opponents particularly resented the queen's efforts on behalf of Hawaiian women. Liliʻuokalani's attempts to strengthen the monarchy also meant strengthening her political power as a woman. Liliʻuokalani had courted other projects to improve the lives of Hawaiian women in an increasingly Americanized culture. She was a member of the "Kaahumanu Society," a group of high-ranking *aliʻi* women who met "to preserve the old traditions and customs and especially to recognize the strength of womanhood." Liliuokalani planned to open a bank for Hawaiian women and a college for Hawaiian girls.[32]

One of Lili'uokalani's favorite projects was Kawaiaha'o Seminary in Honolulu, a boarding school for Hawaiian girls. Founded in 1865 by Charlotte and Luther Gulick, the son of American missionaries to the Hawaiian Islands, the school grew quickly and was supported by missionary descendants.[33]

As the seminary progressed, it sought the support of the government, receiving financial aid from King Kalākaua beginning in 1876. Similarly, Lili'uokalani created the Lili'uokalani Education Society in 1886, which by the 1890s supported twenty-seven students. Lili'uokalani also financed five students from her personal resources, including her daughter, Lydia Aholo.[34]

Lili'uokalani encouraged other Hawaiian women to take interest in the education of "young girls of their own race whose parents would be unable to given them advantages." As a child, Lili'uokalani had attended a missionary boarding school, learned English, and witnessed the population of her country achieve one of the highest literacy rates in the world. While the early American missionaries had taught Hawaiians a written Hawaiian language, Lili'uokalani believed the English language necessary for all native Hawaiians to "detect the purpose of each line and word" in the designs of foreigners. The missionaries had taught English to Lili'uokalani and other high ali'i to help them govern in a colonizing world. Lili'uokalani believed all Hawaiians should have the same knowledge, in order to understand the mechanisms foreigners applied to Hawaiian government and commerce as means to get their way.[35]

Despite Queen Lili'uokalani's personal support for native girls' education, many Hawaiian daughters lost the opportunity to understand the political significance of their turbulent times and instead received the education and values brought to them by American teachers who traveled to the islands in the 1880s and 1890s. The teachers brought with them a clear commitment to patriarchal colonialism, as well as their own place within it.[36]

Learning and Labor

During the late nineteenth century, progressive educators in the Hawaiian Islands embraced the concept of "manual education," which Samuel Chapman Armstrong, the son of American missionaries to the islands, most famously adopted at the Hampton Normal and Industrial School in Virginia after the American Civil War. In noting the "similar" condition between African Americans and Hawaiians, Armstrong convinced educative leaders, such as Bernice Pauahi Bishop, as well as Armstrong's fellow missionary descendants who held trusteeships at numerous privately funded Hawaiian schools, to embrace practical education and normal (teacher) training for native Hawaiians. In a developing wage economy, manual training seemed to Progressive Era Americans exactly what Hawaiian children needed. As a result, Christian donors looked to Oberlin College, a Congregationalist college that embraced practical and normal training, when hiring Kawaiahaʻo's teachers.[37]

Founded by two Congregational ministers in 1833, Oberlin College in Ohio was the first coeducational college in the United States. Its stated goal was to elevate women by "bringing within the reach of the misjudged and neglected sex all the instructive privileges which have unreasonably distinguished the leading sex from theirs." The Oberlin founders wished to train teachers and ministers to reach the western United States. Students were not charged tuition. Instead they worked on campus to support the institution. From the beginning, Oberlin also was open to Black students, making the college an early and powerful site for abolitionist activity. Graduates such as Lucy Stone, founder of the American Women Suffrage Association, and Antoinette Brown, who later joined her, continued Oberlin's countercultural influence after the Civil War.[38]

Oberlin graduates were ready for new professional opportunities after the Civil War, and teaching in overseas boarding schools was one of the few opportunities that Christian missionary organizations offered to single women who had graduated from college. By 1890 five of the eight teachers at Kawaiahaʻo Seminary were Oberlin graduates. All eight teachers were white. While normal training meant preparing native girls to teach in schools after graduation, Armstrong's concept of racial uplift meant that generations of native teachers would continue to teach native students how to work in agriculture and industry, rather than professional fields, such as medicine, law, and higher education. "Thus," Kalani Beyer writes, "even before Hawaiʻi was annexed in 1898, American colonization was well advanced."[39]

By 1890 Kawaiahaʻo Seminary had close to 150 students, with the growth, in part, fueled by the seminary's success in placing graduates into teaching, sewing, clerical, and agricultural occupations. Kawaiahaʻo Seminary from its outset included manual education, such as housekeeping, cooking, and sewing, but it also provided a classical curriculum and English-language instruction like Lili'uokalani had received and wanted for her people. The curriculum at Kawaiaha'o included math, geography, English, and physical education. The girls were forbidden to speak in their native Hawaiian language.[40]

The young American teachers brought their racial superiority with them, and they did not hide it from their pupils. The teachers had little incentive to learn Hawaiian ways. In the words of Carol Chin, "Their own identities resisted hybridization and remained proudly American and Christian."[41] Teachers refused to eat poi at Hawaiian luau celebrations and required their students to use spoons for traditional Hawaiian finger foods. Teachers referred to their students as "stupid," "fat," "dirty," and "disgusting" and mocked their attempts to speak English. Teachers also disciplined students by locking them in dark closets and rooms. "I am to unlock my dormitory and let certain girls out who get supper. The rest remain caged," one teacher wrote.[42]

More disturbingly, Kawaiaha'o teachers relied on corporal punishment. After beating a student with a whip, teacher Carrie Winter wrote her fiancé, "I am really gaining the power of keeping them down." Winter added, "I don't think, Carl, you will ever know what that means till you have worked among a people so few years removed from barbarism as these are."[43]

Kawaiaha'o teachers were dismissive of Hawaiian geography, history, and government. Winter required her geography students to locate on a map the principal rivers and cities of states such as Arkansas and grew frustrated when they could not. Winter apparently was ignorant of the fact that ancient Hawaiian geographers could site hundreds of stars by memory and taught their children to learn the earth's geography in reference to the Pacific Ocean. Winter instead concluded that the girls had a "natural antipathy" for the subject.[44]

Teachers also derided the Hawaiian monarchy. One proudly asserted that she refused to address Queen Lili'uokalani as "Your Majesty," nor "did I rise when she left the room." The attitudes and actions of American teachers toward their Hawaiian students were nothing short of physical and emotional abuse. The teachers' open derision of the young girls included direct attempts to wipe out their Hawaiian culture.[45]

Instead of Hawaiian history, culture, and language, native students described, almost singularly, the moral and religious instruction they received at the seminary. Beginning each day with Bible class, students memorized

Bible passages weekly and were required to attend Wednesday night prayer meetings and Sunday morning services. The seminary diligently worked to fulfill the primary mission of the school: "to convert Hawaiian girls to Christianity." In such an environment it is surprising that students could learn, let alone thrive. At least one student died. Some students ran away. "It was stay in the seminary and die," one runaway stated. Another set the school on fire.[46]

Certainly teachers believed they were fulfilling their mission at an important moment in Hawaiian history. By the late 1880s many whites in the islands viewed the monarchy as retreating from its earlier acceptance of American missionary influence. In 1886 Kawaiahaʻo Board of Trustee president Charles Hyde refused to allow students to attend King Kalākaua's fiftieth birthday party, believing the king was "seeking the overthrow of Christian institutions." Hyde called those siding with the king "on the side in favor of heathenism and indecency." Kawaiahaʻo teachers agreed with him.[47]

Until the revolution, Queen Liliʻuokalani visited the seminary regularly. While teachers welcomed her financial support, it did not mean they accepted her monarchy. Most, if not all, teachers at Kawaiahaʻo supported Liliʻuokalani's overthrow. "I suppose she thinks she is abused," one teacher wrote during the revolution.[48]

The teachers' antipathy toward Liliʻuokalani was striking and shortsighted. Kawaiahaʻo Seminary did not long survive the revolution. White supporters of the school made clear that Kawaiahaʻo would be better off without the "evil" queen, which alienated the school's native supporters. Stripped of her income and crown lands, Liliʻuokalani could no longer support the school through her scholarship fund, and the new revolutionary government ended all tax support for private schools. In 1908 the seminary merged with the Mills Institute for Chinese Boys, Okumura Japanese Boarding School, and Korean Methodist School for Boys and Girls and became the Mid-Pacific Institute, relocating to its present location in Mānoa Valley.[49]

Liliʻuokalani transferred her daughter Lydia Aholo to the new Kamehameha School for Girls in 1894. The Kamehameha Schools for Boys and Girls, funded by the legacy of Liliʻuokalani's *hānai* sister Bernice Pauahi Bishop, provided manual and Christian education in the English language to native Hawaiians. Soon after the revolution, the new government similarly mandated English-language requirements and manual education in all public schools.[50]

Sadly, American progressives in the Hawaiian islands did not seem to mind this educational shift. Oberlin teachers were led by Honolulu's *haole* community in forming their opinions of Lili'uokalani and spent much of their free time socializing with missionary descendants. Sanford Dole later remarked that had native Hawaiians simply gathered against the revolutionaries, the course of Hawaiian history might be different. Lili'uokalani wanted to avoid bloodshed, and it is hard not to wonder what would have happened had American residents in Honolulu, including the teachers at Kawaiaha'o Seminary, stood with the queen and her native supporters against a small group of white men. Would U.S. marines, in the absence of formal military orders, have fired on their fellow American citizens?[51]

Instead, white progressives in the Hawaiian Islands were comfortable accepting nineteenth-century American racial norms and did not (or would not) understand that Lili'uokalani offered her people a *return* to the times of Ka'ahumanu and earlier constitutions when native Hawaiians, including women, had more political power. Standing alongside native students in support of the queen would have violated the teachers' understanding of their own racial superiority. Their feminist ideals, evident in their college papers and personal letters, did not extend to non-white women.[52]

Amid such racial discourse, it is not surprising that American missionary teachers accepted the gender roles defined for them by *haole* in the islands, a role that limited the teachers to training students for wage labor (seen as "racial uplift"). This position meant teaching native Hawaiians to work in jobs far below their white peers. Carrie Winter, for example, wanted to take one of her students back to America to serve as her maid. Like *haole* men, *haole* women in the islands believed Lili'uokalani was *too* independent. Watching the revolution with ambivalence, the teachers ignored their own political potential as progressive white women, relying on knowledge that their sojourn in the islands was temporary. "It is a fact that not another teacher in this school pretends to be attached to this work," Carrie Winter wrote.[53]

Pua Ha'aheo O Ke Aupuni

Many decades would pass before Hawaiian students would recover a sense of what they had lost in the revolution. After U.S. annexation missionary son William Alexander updated his 1891 *Brief History of the Hawaiian People*, writing that the queen's overthrow meant Hawai'i's future was "assured of

19. Kawaiahaʻo Seminary students. "N-3271—Kawaiahao Seminary, girls posed in front of stone wall: Chamberlain House in background. Photograph." Mission Houses Museum Library.

permanent peace and prosperity." Alexander's *Brief History* remained part of the course of study for Hawaiian elementary and secondary schools until the 1920s. A generation of Hawaiian women would not learn what was taken from them with their queen's abdication.[54]

Instead Hawaiian students followed the path of industrial education outlined for Hawaiian schools by the revolutionaries and successive U.S. territorial governments. As president of the Hawaiian Board of Education, William Alexander boasted that schools were instilling "habits of obedience" into the "rising generation." What a far cry from ABCFM missionary Amos Cooke's charge to teachers in 1848. As principal of the Royal School, attended by Liliʻuokalani and other high *aliʻi* children, Cooke implored teachers to respect their Hawaiian students. "Before long they will perhaps become our chiefs," Cooke wrote, "and the teachers perhaps of our own children." Clearly the fragile friendships between Hawaiian *aliʻi* and the American missionaries of an earlier era had been broken by successor generations of *haole*.[55]

As the last monarch of either Tahiti or Hawaiʻi, Liliʻuokalani was also the one most shaped by Euro-American contact. She was a devout Chris-

20. Lili'uokalani, ca. 1913,
by Robert K. Bonine.
Queen Liliuokalani
Photograph Exhibition.
Hawai'i State Archives.

tian, valued the English language, and submitted to constitutional law. In exchange, she lost her status, income, and lands and lived the last two decades of her life in virtual poverty. During the first decade of the twentieth century, Lili'uokalani traveled to the United States five times to protest the loss of her crown lands. They were never restored. In 1912, nearly twenty years after the revolution, the Territorial Government of Hawaii began paying Lili'uokalani an annual pension of $12,000. The government kept her *ali'i* lands, which were valued at $20 million. Lili'uokalani died in 1917 at the age of seventy-nine.[56]

Despite these humiliations, Lili'uokalani demonstrated enormous resilience. She applied the *palapala* to argue her side of the revolution by publishing *Hawaii's Story by Hawaii's Queen* in 1898. Her memoir remains in print. Lili'uokalani used her Hawaiian *aloha* (goodwill) to graciously receive into her home numerous visitors requesting financial aid, supplying what she could. She raised three *hānai* children. Lili'uokalani also left behind a trust for poor and orphaned children. The Lili'uokalani Trust now serves over ten thousand children, giving preference to those of native Hawaiian ancestry. "*Pua ha'aheo o ke aupuni*" (cherished flower of the nation) was composed by Lili'uokalani for her niece Ka'iulani in 1877. Lili'uokalani could not have known how perfectly the name would reflect her own relationship to her people. The *mana* of Hawai'i's last queen is felt in the islands today.[57]

Conclusion

To All the Queens

Luhi wahine ʻia.
[Labored over by a woman.]
—HAWAIIAN PROVERB

Purea, ʻAimata, Kaʻahumanu, and Liliʻuokalani occupied vibrant political roles in Polynesian societies prior to formal European and American colonization. Each woman pressed her society toward increasing the political leadership of women in issues of religion and state, even when unsupported by powerful chiefs and foreigners operating within her borders. The fact the Tahitian and Hawaiian kingdoms ultimately lost their independence and native women receded into the background of colonial regimes does not negate the power these women exercised during the eighteenth and nineteenth centuries. Showing themselves astute in recognizing the challenges at hand, the women alternated between native and foreign objectives in ways that preserved their nations' independence for as long as possible. As political leaders the women are astounding. As women operating in a patriarchal, imperial world, they are unparalleled.

Word

When Liliʻuokalani abdicated her throne, the revolutionaries required her to sign the document as "Liliʻuokalani Dominis," a name that she had never taken and an action she believed rendered the document invalid. "There is not, and never was, within the range of my knowledge, any such person as Liliʻuokalani Dominis," Liliʻuokalani declared, rejecting the American custom that a wife must legally adopt her husband's surname.[1]

It may seem obvious that white foreigners utilized arguments of gender to justify revolution against 'Aimata and Lili'uokalani, but Europeans and Americans also aided Purea, 'Aimata, Ka'ahumanu, and Lili'uokalani when it suited their purposes. Of course, both are true, which means that race, religion, culture, and gender were all salient yet malleable factors in how foreigners viewed Tahitian and Hawaiian leadership. Larger international politics were also at play, leading to English, French, and American displays of power that were unassailable for native peoples. The stories of these women are strikingly similar despite spanning more than one century. Their experiences also point to long legacies of trauma for the Tahitian and Hawaiian people. Myths persist regarding Polynesian cultures, while the knowledge of Polynesian women holding political leadership is lost. If we look past an archive dominated by white men, perhaps these women can speak as loudly today as they did in their lifetime.

The *palapala* (*parau* in Tahitian), or written word, is at the heart of each woman's story. The captains and crew who met Purea and her people sexualized them as caricatures to British and French audiences. Their lack of understanding of Tahitian language, religion, and culture allowed European men to rewrite their own desires and fears onto Tahitian women, laying the groundwork for missionary involvement. Thomas Haweis, a cofounder of the London Missionary Society (LMS), recorded that it was Hawkesworth's published accounts of Cook's voyages that "excited in his mind a strong desire" to send English Protestant missionaries to Tahiti. The American Sunday School Union published Henry 'Ōpūkaha'ia's memoir in the United States in 1818 after the young Hawaiian immigrant died of typhus. 'Ōpūkaha'ia's terrifying *palapala* describing Hawaiian religion, his subsequent conversion to Christianity, and his plan to return to the islands as a missionary directly influenced the first group of American Protestant missionaries to travel to the islands the following year.[2]

More importantly, travelers' stories about Polynesian islands incited decades of eager explorers to visit Tahiti and Hawai'i. They carried with them epidemics. Native Hawaiians referred to such illnesses as becoming "shippy," in reference to the naval and merchant vessels that brought disease. The overwhelming majority of the population in both the Society and Hawaiian Islands died from these devastating imports.[3]

For Ka'ahumanu, the *palapala* was a way to share *mana* with the American missionaries who came from a place possessing trade goods, weapons, and Christianity. Kaʻahumanu was responsible for creating, in a strikingly short amount of time, one of the most literate cultures in the world. "We want literacy, it may make us wise," she wrote.[4]

ʻAimata could not read or write. She did not think it was necessary. She was the highest *ariʻi* in Tahiti. Yet her inability to understand the nuances and legalities of the French documents she was compelled by threat of cannon to sign led to the loss of her country. As one Tahitian chief wrote to the British government, "We did not know what was written neither did we know well its contents. We signed our names to the letter as it were in the Dark." He further pleaded: "Have the letter considered null and void."[5]

Great Britain was unwilling to intercede against France, viewing the Tahitian government as having entered into a legitimate treaty through the *parau*. "The letter in which French protection was solicited was, by her own will and act, signed by the Queen," Lord Aberdeen wrote to George Pritchard, ignoring the moral complications created by forcing an illiterate queen to give written consent to her overthrow, or coercing a group of chiefs to sign a treaty in the queen's name while she was giving birth to her child.[6]

Liliʻuokalani believed strongly in the English *palapala*. She thought her formal surrender to the United States and the subsequent Blount report would carry the *mana* to reinstate her throne. She believed that agreements signed by previous Hawaiian monarchs with Great Britain, France, and the United States rendered hostile acts of aggression, such as annexation, a violation of international law.[7]

So, too, did the Hawaiian people who sent to President McKinley in 1897 a 550-page document titled "*Palapala Hoopii Kua Hoohui Aina*" (Petitions against Annexation), in which native Hawaiians protested U.S. annexation. The document today is housed in the U.S. National Archives. Liliʻuokalani had been taught from a young age to respect biblical and civil law. After U.S. annexation in 1898, Liliʻuokalani concluded, "The doctrine that might makes right seems to prevail."[8]

ʻAimata and Liliʻuokalani also understood the power of the *spoken* word. Each utilized the older tradition that, too, contained *mana*. In the face of French and American threats, ʻAimata and Liliʻuokalani issued proclamations to their people to wait peacefully for justice. Their spoken word *created* the power of peaceful resistance, but their *mana* was so powerful that French and American diplomats feared unrest. Yet both speeches expressed optimism, not violence. "Return to your homes peaceably and quietly and continue to look toward me, and I will look toward you," Lili'uokalani told Hawaiians who had gathered to see her new constitution promulgated. "Britain will not cast us off," 'Aimata declared. "Do not on any account cause evil to grow."[9]

Unfortunately, the foreign response to the women's spoken word influenced the trajectory of Tahitian and Hawaiian history. The French colonial government called 'Aimata's proclamation an "act of defiance" that encouraged the Tahitian people to participate with the British in the overthrow of French control. The French governor of the Society Islands exiled 'Aimata and forbade her to set foot on Tahiti.[10] The *haole* revolutionaries in Hawai'i interpreted Lili'uokalani's announcement as a signal she would promulgate the constitution without the support of her cabinet or the legislature. Sanford Dole called her address a "vehement" promise to "carry out her scheme" and immediately began the revolution.[11]

Action

Nineteenth-century English and American missionaries brought their cultural interpretation of the *palapala* to the islands, believing that scriptural injunctions made women subordinate to men. Women were descendants of Eve, subject to whims, deceptions, and ignorance. Missionary men hoped to contain them in domestic spheres, and missionary women helped their husbands do so. Women should not "meddle with politics," missionary fathers taught their sons. The biblical curse precluded a woman's involvement in governance, according to missionary interpretation of the *palapala*.[12]

Even when faced with contrary Polynesian practices, the missionaries *would not yield*. Rufus Anderson, secretary of the American Board of Commissioners for Foreign Missions (ABCFM), corresponded regularly with his LMS counterpart, William Ellis, and explained proper Christian gender roles: "The centre of [the missionary wife's] appropriate sphere is, indeed, within the domestic circle. The care of her household is the duty, to which all others must be subservient. This is the scriptural view of her peculiar responsibilities *under all possible circumstances*."[13]

American missionaries placed their theological understanding of gender into Hawaiian law. Legal changes defining land use, taxes, and property ownership reflected the missionaries' commitment to wage-based capitalism and separate gender spheres. In Tahiti, English missionaries encouraged laws against adultery, which counteracted traditional marriage agreements that were nonbinding and did not transfer property ownership. All Tahitian subjects were required to pay an annual tax (called a "subscription") to the London Missionary Society.[14]

In these transcultural encounters Tahitian and Hawaiian women *acted*, attempting to join their *mana* with powerful foreigners and create new genealogical lines. They faced counteraction as a result. American missionaries sought to rewrite existing genealogies, renaming Kaʻahumanu "Elisabeth" and Liliʻuokalani "Lydia" at their baptisms. Both were biblical names. British explorers and officials ignored Tahitian female rulers, referring to Purea as the "*Dolphin*'s queen" and ʻAimata as "Pōmare," after her father. The *haole* revolutionaries in the Hawaiian Islands negated centuries of genealogical and matriarchal history by referring to Liliʻuokalani as "Mrs. Dominis."[15]

Despite their treatment by foreigners who defied their laws and missionaries who rewrote them, Tahitian and Hawaiian queens believed that they were equal to other living monarchs. "Sister Sovereigns" was how ʻAimata and Liliʻuokalani viewed their relationship with Queen Victoria. There is no evidence that Victoria felt the same. In June 1887 Liliʻuokalani and her sister-in-law Kapiʻolani traveled to London to participate in Queen Victoria's Golden Jubilee. They were admired by the press for their "regal" deportment even though, writers noted, they were "swarthy" and came from a "tolerably civilized" nation.[16]

Victoria met with Liliʻuokalani and Kapiʻolani. Liliʻuokalani was enchanted by the national celebrations for the monarch, believing Victoria "a woman whose name is respected and loved." In fact, the jubilee was designed to showcase the immense power the British Empire held over the colonized world, and Victoria was ambivalent, if not hostile, toward her required participation. Meanwhile Honolulu was in rebellion. *Haole* businessmen and sugar interests had forced Kalakaua to sign the Bayonet Constitution. When Liliʻuokalani and Kapiʻolani received word of the political unrest, they immediately returned home.[17]

Force

Missionary (mis)interpretation of the Bible had international ramifications. Catholic priests arrived in the Hawaiian Islands in 1827 and in Tahiti in 1833. In both places the Catholic Church hoped to establish a mission, but Kaʻahumanu and ʻAimata, under missionary direction, expelled them. The rulers' actions prompted the Roman Catholic Church to investigate the treatment of Catholics living on both islands. The French government sent Commodore du Petit-Thouars and his sixty-gun frigate, the *Venus*, to Tahiti to demand reparations from 'Aimata and force her to grant France the most favored nation status it shared with Great Britain. In 1838 Captain Laplace on board the *Artemise* landed in Tahiti to make further demands on behalf of the Roman Catholic Church before traveling on to the Hawaiian Islands in 1839 to impose upon the Hawaiian monarchy equal treatment for both France and the Roman Catholic religion.[18]

By this time Britain, France, and the United States each had naval vessels stationed at Valparaiso, Chile, in order to respond quickly to threats against the lives and property of their nationals living in the Pacific. All three nations dealt with rogue captains and nebulous claims of aggression made by citizens living abroad.[19]

Officers and crew aboard these ships also demanded prostitutes. Few seemed aware that they had helped create the industry in the first place. When French Commander Louis de Bougainville arrived in Tahiti in 1768, one junior officer on board the *Boudeuse* noticed that young Tahitian girls often wept when offered to the sailors by their elders. Bougainville, however, was ecstatic. "We are offered all the young girls. Our white skin delights them, they express their admiration in this regard in the most expressive manner," the commander wrote. Bougainville called Tahiti "New Cythera," after the goddess Aphrodite.[20]

'Aimata would later protest to King Louis-Philippe that members of the French navy had "seized" married women from the Tahitian shore and raped them aboard their ships, a much different depiction of "New Cythera" than French romantics wanted to believe. "I am afflicted for my lands," 'Aimata wrote to Queen Victoria. "I am grieved."[21]

England, France, and the United States each strategized over annexing islands in the Pacific. In 1843 British captain George Paulet aboard the *Carysfort* took possession of the Hawaiian Islands without the direction of his government. He alleged Hawaiian abuses toward British nationals living in the islands. Embarrassed, the British government sent Admiral Richard Thomas to restore the Hawaiian flag. As a result of Paulet's actions, Great Britain was forced to sign a treaty with the Hawaiian Kingdom and an agreement with France guaranteeing that the British government would respect the independence of the islands. This fiasco for the British government occurred at the same moment 'Aimata requested British aid in nullifying the treaty she had signed with France. Britain declined.[22]

The British government did, however, expect Louis-Phillippe to nullify 'Aimata's forced abdication, just as Admiral Thomas had nullified the British overthrow of Kamehameha III. The French king agreed, although he kept Tahiti as a protectorate, and France ultimately annexed the island after 'Aimata's death. Sanford Dole threatened to appeal to Great Britain for protection if the United States interfered with the *haole* revolution and new provisional government. Lili'uokalani called his warning "absurd." The British Foreign Office planned to keep New Zealand and Australia at all costs. All of these events show the international and interwoven nature of foreign policy in the Pacific during the nineteenth century.[23]

LMS missionary John Orsmond was the first to point out that arguments between Catholics and Protestants in Tahiti could have long-term negative consequences for the Tahitian people. However, Lord Henry Grey, speaking for the Whig Party in the English Parliament, was not ready to concede the point. French occupation of Tahiti "was calculated to cause considerable apprehension in the minds of many persons in this country who took a great interest in the welfare of these islanders," Grey argued. Grey advocated continued support for 'Aimata and the LMS missionaries even at the cost of war. Ultimately Grey lost the debate while Queen Victoria fretted over the negative press the Whigs had caused her government.[24]

Yet the dangers to 'Aimata and Lili'uokalani were real. 'Aimata feared assassination, as did Lili'uokalani, who wrote that spies "prowl about ... at dead of night, equipped with loaded revolvers and belts full of cartridges." Rumors swirled that the provisional government would deport the Hawaiian queen. The French colonial government exiled 'Aimata. Both queens felt responsible for their nations and attempted to keep their people safe in the midst of their own fears. Both women felt alone. Lobbying against annexation in Washington DC, Lili'uokalani wrote that she had no one but herself to represent her people. Half a century earlier, 'Aimata wept that "she had not one person left to comfort me in my trials."[25]

Conflict

From the beginning, France's entry into the Pacific trade created international conflict. French wine and brandy, specific articles of trade interest to the French government, horrified English and American Protestant missionaries, who believed alcoholism was the primary factor forcing demographic decline in both islands. Additional treaty requirements opening the islands to all forms of religious proselytization meant an influx of Mormon missionaries into the Hawaiian Islands and Catholic priests into Tahiti. LMS missionaries ultimately conceded the Society Islands to France, marking the end of their involvement in Tahiti and, according to the annals of the London Missionary Society, a national failure for England.[26]

English and American missionary leadership were in communication during this period. William Ellis and Rufus Anderson discussed the Catholic missionaries as a "dire threat" to Protestant interests. They also debated their complicit relationships with Indigenous rulers who asked the missionaries for "advice on matters of state." George Pritchard in Tahiti and Gerrit Judd in Hawai'i chose politics over missions, hoping to earn more money. Each began a complicated journey in which they represented personal, missionary, and royal interests.[27]

Nevertheless, Ka'ahumanu, 'Aimata, and Lili'uokalani remained committed to Christian authority in law and culture. "I and he [Kamehameha III] whom I have brought up have indeed carried the word of our Lord through from Hawaii to Kauai," Ka'ahumanu reported to the ABCFM in Boston in 1831. Lili'uokalani later appealed to the United States "from whom my ancestors learned the Christian religion" in protesting the *haole* revolutionaries, just as 'Aimata appealed to her co-Christian European sovereigns to restore her throne. And just as Victoria refused to dialogue with 'Aimata, so, too, did President McKinley refuse to meet with Lili'uokalani.[28]

Publicly Lili'uokalani repeated the reason given by McKinley for declining to meet privately with her in the months after his March 1897 inauguration: the president's "pressing public duties" precluded a meeting. Privately, Lili'uokalani pressed her case to McKinley. "Four-fifths of the voters of Hawaii are disenfranchised," Lili'uokalani wrote the president. "The only way that the Hawaiian people can obtain a hearing in the councils of this great power with whom for nearly one hundred years they have been allied in terms of closest friendship is that you, as the chief magistrate of the United States, should admit me as one of my people, to a conference."[29]

Lili'uokalani's appeal failed. Three months into his presidency, McKinley sent Secretary of State John Sherman to meet with the pro-annexation delegation from the Hawaiian Republic. McKinley signed an annexation treaty and introduced it to the U.S. Senate later that same day.[30]

The American public, too, had been swayed by the many pro-annexationist arguments regularly represented in the press. As Lili'uokalani observed, "with few exceptions, the press has seemed to favor the extinction of Hawaiian sovereignty." Not only biased, Lili'uokalani noted, "[the press] has declined to publish letters from myself and friends conveying correct information." Americans also may have been deceived by the Hawaiian Senate's vote to "ratify" U.S. annexation of the Hawaiian Republic in September 1897. The vote itself was meaningless, no more than a stunt by *haole* members of the chamber who hoped to mislead Americans into believing that the disenfranchised, native Hawaiian public supported annexation.[31]

The cultural divide between Hawaiian and American understandings of Oceanic history was vast. The same held true for Tahitians and the British Foreign Office. While Polynesian rulers looked to early trade agreements with foreign nations as moral guideposts for their future relations with Europe and the United States, European and American governments seized the past as a springboard for new agendas. The influence of the earliest English and American missionaries, naval officers, and consuls to Tahiti and Hawai'i had enormous, long-term effects upon Polynesian concepts of gender and religion. The first white visitors to the islands began the trajectory toward French and U.S. annexation and aided the European and American belief that civilization and progress were the unique gifts of white nations to the rest of the world. The reality that missionaries did not support the foreign policy interests of their respective nation-states fundamentally worked against native rulers as they embraced Christianity and the nationals who brought it but were denied equal rites of friendship by the missionaries' powerful countries of origin. In neither England nor the United States did women's rights advocates equate their own lack of the vote to 'Aimata or Lili'uokalani's loss of political sovereignty. The idea that Polynesian women may have been more advanced than they were was too foreign a concept to consider.[32]

Mana

Many have written about precontact Polynesia, European exploration, and nineteenth-century colonialism. Others have reworked the archives to incorporate feminist theory into groundbreaking revisions of previous perceptions of the past. A few have applied theory to the use of power in foreign relations when morality is at stake.[33]

Was annexation of Hawai'i or Tahiti a foregone conclusion when Britain, France, and the United States considered the importance of Pacific islands to their nineteenth-century naval and trade networks? Queen Victoria, George Pritchard, President McKinley, and Sanford Dole certainly did not think so. In England, Protestant supporters of the London Missionary Society wrote petitions on 'Aimata's behalf to Sir Robert Peel and the Conservative Party. Pritchard rallied British naval captains to 'Aimata's cause and traveled to England to meet with the British government. Lord Grey and the Whig Party defended the Protestant missionary cause in Parliament. Victoria later told her uncle that England and France had been very close to war.[34]

In the Hawaiian Islands, Sanford Dole was willing to go to war with the United States to protect the revolution, while President McKinley debated how best to accomplish ratification of the annexation treaty he signed in 1897. Lili'uokalani traveled to Washington DC, believing her presence there the only reason the U.S. Senate delayed voting on the treaty. McKinley distanced himself from her.[35]

When the United States went to war against Spain in Cuba and the Philippines in April 1898, McKinley and pro-annexationists in Congress utilized a joint resolution, not a treaty, to accomplish their goal, fearing they lacked the two-thirds majority required for treaty ratification in the Senate. The anti-imperialist movement in the United States comprised a complicated coalition of trade protectionists, racists, and moralists, a group that tended to be unwieldy but powerful. The Newlands Resolution, annexing the Hawaiian Islands, passed the U.S. House and Senate comfortably, although the Senate margin proved to be a razor-sharp, two-thirds majority.[36]

Placed into their proper context of the political unknown, the actions of Purea, 'Aimata, Ka'ahumanu, and Lili'uokalani become more powerful. How many have chosen to risk death, poverty, or permanent loss of reputation to fight against systemic injustice when stronger forces were against them? Such individuals are usually elevated in history as those worthy of emulation. Purea defied the chiefs, 'Aimata the French, Ka'ahumanu the gods, and Lili'uokalani the *haole*. Even more, these women defied the constant racial and gender hatred directed toward them by white men and women who were supported by their more powerful nations. These Polynesian *transcolonial queens* ignited their *mana* through both word and action, creating a profound legacy for their people. "It is for them that I would give the last drop of my blood," Liliʻuokalani wrote about her people in 1898. "It is for them that I would spend, nay, am spending, everything belonging to me."[37] Unquestionably, the lives of these four chiefs add richly to the collective, living *mana* of women in governance and international affairs and to our understanding of contested leadership, cultural difference, and the contingencies of political power.

for one of them who has been
willed

This is my speech to you
help me speedily, that my cap
tivity may soon pass away — do
not leave me in Bondage in a
strange land, but aid me and
restore me to my kingdom in
my own lands, with uprightness,
with peace, and with my Sovereign
power upon me, and all will be
well.

This is my earnest desire —
stretch out quickly towards me
your powerful hand, that my
afflictions and trouble may soon
pass away with this Captivity and
death, and all will be well.

May you be saved
Pomare

Rurutu Sep 1. 1844.

21. Pōmare to Victoria, September 1, 1844. South Seas Journals and
Letters, 1796–1899, Inventory of Letters from Missionaries in Oceania,
Special Collections and Archives, University of San Diego Library.

Appendix A

Partial Letter from Pōmare to
Queen Victoria (1844)

This is my speech to you.
Help me speedily that my captivity may soon pass away. Do
not leave me in Bondage in a
strange land but aid me and
restore me to my Kingdom in
my own land with uprightness,
and peace, and with my Sovereign
power upon me, and all will be
well.

    This is my earnest desire—
Stretch out quickly towards me
your powerful hand, that my
afflictions and trouble may soon
pass away with this Captivity and
death, and all will be well.

    May you be saved
                Pomare

Raiatea Sep 1, 1844

Appendix B

*Queen Lili'uokalani's Formal
Protest to the United States against
the Annexation Treaty (1897)*

I, *Liliuokalani of Hawaii*, by the Will of God named heir-apparent on the tenth day of April, A.D. 1877, and by the grace of God Queen of the Hawaiian Islands on the seventeenth day of January, A.D. 1893, do hereby protest against the ratification of a certain treaty, which, so I am informed, has been signed at Washington by Messrs, Hatch, Thurston, and Kinney, purporting to cede those Islands to the territory and dominion of the United States. I declare such a treaty to be an act of wrong toward the native and part-native people of Hawaii, an invasion of the rights of the ruling chiefs, in violation of international rights both toward my people and toward friendly nations with whom they have made treaties, the perpetuation of the fraud whereby the constitutional government was overthrown, and, finally, an act of gross injustice to me.

BECAUSE the official protests made by me on the seventeenth day of January, 1893, to the so-called Provisional Government was signed by me, and received by said government with the assurance that the case was referred to the United States of America for arbitration. BECAUSE that protest and my communications to the United States Government immediately thereafter expressly declare that I yielded my authority to the forces of the United States in order to avoid bloodshed, and because I recognized the futility of a conflict with so formidable a power.

BECAUSE the President of the United States, the Secretary of State, and an envoy commissioned by them reported in official documents that my government was unlawfully coerced by the forces, diplomatic and naval, of the United States; that I was at the date of their investigations the constitutional ruler of my people. BECAUSE neither the above-named commission nor the government which sends it has ever received any such authority from the registered voters of Hawaii, but derives its assumed powers from the so-called committee of public safety, organized on or about the seventeenth-day of January, 1893, said committee being composed largely of persons claiming American citizenship, and not one single Hawaiian was a member thereof, or in any way participated in the demonstration leading to its existence.

BECAUSE my people, about forty thousand in number, have in no way been consulted by those, three thousand in number, who claim the right to destroy the independence of Hawaii. My people constitute four-fifths of the legally qualified voters of Hawaii, and excluding those imported for the demands of labor, about the same proportion of the inhabitants.

BECAUSE said treaty ignores, not only the civic rights of my people, but, further, the hereditary property of their chiefs. Of the 4,000,000 acres composing the territory said treaty offers to annex, 1,000,000 or 915,000 acres has in no way been heretofore recognized as other than the private property of the constitutional monarch, subject to a control in no way differing from other items of a private estate.

BECAUSE it is proposed by said treaty to confiscate said property, technically called the crown lands, those legally entitled thereto, either now or in succession, receiving no consideration whatever for estates, their title to which has been always undisputed, and which is legitimately in my name at this date.

BECAUSE said treaty ignores, not only all professions of perpetual amity and good faith made by the United States in former treaties with the sovereigns representing the Hawaiian people, but all treaties made by those sovereigns with other and friendly powers, and it is thereby in violation of international law.

BECAUSE, by treating with the parties claiming at this time the right to cede said territory of Hawaii, the Government of the United States receives such territory from the hands of those whom its own magistrates (legally elected by the people of the United States, and in office in 1893) pronounced fraudulently in power and unconstitutionally ruling Hawaii.

Therefore I, *Liliuokalani of Hawaii*, do hereby call upon the President of that nation, to whom alone I yielded my property and my authority, to withdraw said treaty (ceding said Islands) from further consideration. I ask the honorable Senate of the United States to decline to ratify said treaty, and I implore the people of this great and good nation, from whom my ancestors learned the Christian religion, to sustain their representatives in such acts of justice and equity as may be in accord with the principles of their fathers, and to the Almighty Ruler of the universe, to him who judgeth righteously, I commit my cause.

Done at Washington, District of Columbia, United States of America, this seventeenth day of June, in the year eighteen hundred and ninety-seven.

Notes

Introduction

1. Excellent sources on precontact Tahiti include the oral history recorded by Adams, *Tahiti*; the notes of missionary John Orsmond compiled by his granddaughter in Henry, *Ancient Tahiti*; and Salmond, *Aphrodite's Island*.

2. Primary sources on early English and American missionary contact include Ellis, *London Missionary Society*; and Bingham, *Residence*. The London Missionary Society archives are held at the National Library of Australia and University of San Diego Library. The American Board of Commissioners for Foreign Missions archives are held at Harvard University.

3. For a discussion of English trade routes and exchanges, see Maud, "Tahitian Pork Trade"; and Newell, *Trading Nature*.

4. See Thigpen's insightful analysis of American missionary contact with Kaʻahumanu in Thigpen, *Island Queens*.

5. Much of ʻAimata's correspondence is held with the London Missionary Society's correspondence at the National Library of Australia. Liliʻuokalani published her own record of the revolution. See Liliuokalani, *Hawaii's Story*. On the role of foreign epidemics in Polynesia, see Igler, *Great Ocean*.

6. For a discussion on the intercourse of race and gender by English explorers, see Wilson, "Empire, Gender, and Modernity," 14–45. On colonial America and racial constructs, see Morgan, "Encounters," 42–78.

7. On early missionary societies, see Gunson, *Messengers of Grace*; and Andrew, *Rebuilding the Christian Commonwealth*.

8. The Hawaiian Mission Houses Historic Site and Archives in Honolulu contains the archives of the Hawaiian Mission Children's Society and the Hawaiian Evangelical Association, which contain numerous documents written by Christian supporters of the overthrow of Queen Liliʻuokalani. A French perspective of the French-Tahitian War comes from Moerenhout, *Voyages aux îles*. Moerenhout was the French consul in Tahiti during the French takeover of the island.

9. See Newbury, *Tahiti Nui*; Oliver, *Ancient Tahitian Society*; Gunson, "Sacred Women Chiefs," 139–72; and Salmond, *Aphrodite's Island*.

10. Early narratives include Kuykendall, *Hawaiian Kingdom*; and Sahlins, *Historical Metaphors*. For more recent evaluations, see Thigpen, *Island Queens*; and Arista, *Kingdom and the Republic*. Missionary women are discussed in Grimshaw, *Paths of Duty*; and Zwiep, *Pilgrim Path*.

11. The Blount Report, which President Grover Cleveland commissioned, sided with Liliʻuokalani. Lord Palmerston, writing for the British Foreign Office, informed its consul in Tahiti, George Pritchard, that Britain would not intervene in a French protectorate of the island. See Blount, *Affairs in Hawaii*. The records of the Foreign Office for nineteenth-century Polynesia are housed at the National Library of Australia and the British Library in London.

12. Prior to European contact, Polynesian chiefs were not called kings or queens. See Handy and Pukui, *Polynesian Family System*, 41.

13. Chang, *World and All the Things*; Druett, *Tupaia*.

14. See Newbury, *Tahiti Nui*; and Oliver, *Ancient Tahitian Society*.

15. Salmond, *Aphrodite's Island*, 2–27.

16. On religion in the Hawaiian Islands, see Kameʻeleihiwa, *Native Land*.

17. Handy and Pukui, *Polynesian Family System*, 41; K. Cook, *Return to Kahiki*, 2–3; J. Cook, *Journals of Captain Cook*.

18. Gunson, "Sacred Women Chiefs," 139; Linnekin, *Sacred Queens*, 16.

19. Gunson, "Sacred Women Chiefs," 142. On Hawaiian rituals, see Valeri, *Kingship and Sacrifice*.

20. Porter, "North American Experience," 345–63.

21. On missionary children, see Manktelow, *Gender, Power and Sexual Abuse*; and Schulz, *Hawaiian by Birth*. On missionary activity, see Gunson, *Messengers of Grace*, 28. Roman Catholics compose roughly half of Christian populations in both French Polynesia and Hawaiʻi. "French Polynesia," *The World Factbook*, February 8, 2021, https://www.cia.gov/the-world-factbook/countries/french-polynesia/#people-and-society; "Hawaii," Pew Research Center, accessed February 14, 2021, https://www.pewforum.org/religious-landscape-study/state/hawaii/.

22. Porter, "North American Experience," 351.

23. Recent environmental histories of nineteenth-century Pacific Ocean trade include Demuth, *Floating Coast*; Melillo, "Making Sea Cucumbers," 449–74; and Ravalli, *Sea Otters*.

24. On the post–Revolutionary War period, see Yokota, *Unbecoming British*.

25. Deckker in Pritchard, *Aggressions*, 17–18.

26. Deckker, in Pritchard, *Aggressions*, 17–18.

27. On informal empire and the nineteenth-century United States, see Tyrrell,

Reforming the World; Conroy-Krutz, *Christian Imperialism*; and Shoemaker, *Pursuing Respect*.

28. On the U.S.-China trade, see Rosenberg, *Spreading the American Dream*. For a history of Pacific Ocean trade, see Matsuda, *Pacific Worlds*.

29. On separate spheres of gender in the nineteenth-century United States, see Cott, *Bonds of Womanhood*; or Welter, "Cult of True Womanhood."

30. Hardwick, "Fractured Domesticity," 1268. See also Yokota, *Unbecoming British*.

31. See Jacobs, *White Mother*; Stoler, *Carnal Knowledge*. See also Merry, *Colonizing Hawai'i*.

32. Chernock, *Right to Rule*, 16–18.

33. On American concepts of manhood, see Hoganson, *Fighting for American Manhood*; and Bederman, *Manliness and Civilization*. On gender and the West, see Herbert, *Gold Rush Manliness*. On American expansion and race, see Lew-Williams, *Chinese Must Go*; and Madley, *American Genocide*.

34. On women's colleges, see Smith, *Transforming Women's Education*; Porterfield, *Mary Lyon*; and Scott, "Ever-Widening Circle," On English and American feminism, see Burton, *Burdens of History*; and Pascoe, *Relations of Rescue*. See also Carey, "Companions in the Wilderness?," 227–48; and Perry, "From 'the Hot-Bed,'" 587–610.

35. On removal, see Jacobs, *White Mother*. On race and education, see Eittreim, *Teaching Empire*; and Coloma, "'Destiny Has Thrown the Negro,'" 496–519. See also Haskins, "Domesticating Colonizers," 1290–301.

36. Oliver, *Ancient Tahitian Society*, 369–74.

37. Malo, *Hawaiian Antiquities*, 113, 275.

38. Kamakau, *Ruling Chiefs of Hawaii*, 238.

39. Reeves-Ellington, "Women, Protestant Missions," 1–16; Manktelow, *Gender, Power and Sexual Abuse*, 54.

40. Hunter first made this argument regarding Progressive missionary women in Hunter, *Gospel of Gentility*. For the Hawaiian context, see Bonura and Day, *American Girl*; and Bonura, *Light*. On Hawaiian missionary men, see K. Cook, *Return to Kahiki*.

41. Manktelow, *Gender, Power and Sexual Abuse*, 53.

1. Purea

1. James Morrison, *Journal of James Morrison on the "Bounty" and at Tahiti, 9 Sept. 1787–1791, Written in 1792*, Mitchell Library, State Library of New South Wales, microfilm 1–42; Adams, *Tahiti*, 182; Gunson, "Great Women," 53, 62, 68.

2. Gunson, "Great Women," 53, 62, 68.

3. Morrison, *Journal*; Adams, *Tahiti*, 101.

4. Adams, *Tahiti*, 40; Wilson, "Empire, Gender, and Modernity," 25. A comprehensive history of Tahiti can be found in Oliver, *Ancient Tahitian Society*.

5. Carrington, *Discovery of Tahiti*, 187; Patel, *Exploration*, 270, 281; Beaglehole, *The Endeavor Journal*, 266.

6. Salmond, *Aphrodite's Island*, 26–28.

7. Salmond, *Aphrodite's Island*, 28–30.

8. Salmond, *Aphrodite's Island*, 28–30.

9. Henry, *Ancient Tahiti*, 231–37; Adams, *Tahiti*, 41.

10. J. M. Orsmond, *The Aori War*, Papers on Tahiti, New South Wales Library Archives.

11. Adams, *Tahiti*, 42.

12. Or, around the year 1762. See Adams, *Tahiti*, 42; Morrison, *Journal*.

13. Adams, *Tahiti*, 42.

14. Adams, *Tahiti*, 42.

15. Morrison, *Journal*.

16. Salmond, *Aphrodite's Island*, 135; Gunson, "Great Women," 55.

17. Beaglehole, *The* Endeavor *Journal*, 303–4.

18. Adams, *Tahiti*, 28–29, 44–46; Henry, *Ancient Tahiti*, 188.

19. Adams, *Tahiti*, 42–44. Morrison called Purea the "regent." See Morrison, *Journal*.

20. Patel, *Exploration*, xx, 251.

21. Salmond, *Aphrodite's Island*, 46–48; Newbury, *Tahiti Nui*, 13; Morrison, *Journal*.

22. Salmond, *Aphrodite's Island*, 50.

23. Patel, *Explorations*, 254; Carrington, *Discovery of Tahiti*, 164.

24. Pate, *Explorations*, 254; Carrington, *Discovery of Tahiti*, 164; Salmond, *Aphrodite's Island*, 56.

25. Carrington, *Discovery of Tahiti*, 187; Patel, *Explorations*, 270–71.

26. Patel, *Explorations*, 270–71.

27. Moerenhout, *Voyages aux îles*, 388–90; Patel, *Explorations*, 270–71.

28. Patel, *Explorations*, 270–71.

29. Adams, *Tahiti*, 50.

30. Carrington, *Discovery of Tahiti*, 206.

31. Carrington, *Discovery of Tahiti*, 207; Patel, *Explorations*, 274.

32. In his unpublished history of Tahiti, London Missionary Society missionary Robert Thomson wrote that Purea's *marae* took two years to build before it was destroyed in 1768. See Robert Thomson, "History of Tahiti" (1815), Records of the London Missionary Society (as filmed by the AJCP), Series, Letters from missionaries in the Society and Hervey Islands and also the Marquesas, Samoan and Sandwich Islands, 1835–1836 (hereafter LMS), National Library of Australia; Morrison, *Journal*. Anne Salmond writes that hair braiding symbolized genealogies, and "Purea was tying Wallis and the British into her lineage." See Salmond, *Aphrodite's Island*, 80.

33. Morrison, *Journal*.

34. Adams wrote: "At all feasts, women and children ate apart from the men, and the boys and girls sat in separate groups" (Adams, *Tahiti*, 177). In his journal Morrison observed: "The Men and Women eat separate, and for this reason each Family has two houses except a Man Chooses to reside in his Wife's house and then each take one end." Morrison also notes: "The Men may partake of any of the Women's Food but must not touch any but what is given them.... No Woman Can eat in a house where a Chief has been, unless she is of the same rank and authority with Him" (Morrison, *Journal*). Robertson recorded that Purea served her guests in their order of rank. See Carrington, *Discovery of Tahiti*, 203–4.

35. Carrington, *Discovery of Tahiti*, 203–4.

36. Patel, *Explorations*, 281.

37. Salmond, *Aphrodite's Island*, 135–36; Gunson, "Great Women," 65.

38. Beaglehole, *The Endeavor Journal*, 304–5; Adams, *Tahiti*, 57.

39. Adams, *Tahiti*, 74–75.

40. Maud, "Tahitian Pork Trade," 178.

41. Salmond, *Aphrodite's Island*, 51; Silva, "Mana Hawai'i," 41.

42. Carrington, *Discovery of Tahiti*, 166.

43. Carrington, *Discovery of Tahiti*, 207; Salmond, *Aphrodite's Island*, 68.

44. See Igler, *Great Ocean*, 43–72.

45. Morrison, *Journal*; Newell, *Trading Nature*, 113; Ellis, *Polynesian Researches*; Ellis, *London Missionary Society*, 360.

46. Carrington, *Discovery of Tahiti*, 211–2; Patel, *Explorations*, 273.

47. Carrington, *Discovery of Tahiti*, 200.

48. Newell, *Trading Nature*, 62.

49. Beaglehole, *The Endeavor Journal*, 266.

50. Newell, *Trading Nature*, 145. See also Patrick O'Brian, *Joseph Banks*; and Fara, *Sex, Botany, & Empire*.

51. See Fara, *Sex, Botany, & Empire*. On the *Bounty*, see C. Alexander, *The Bounty*.

52. Abbott, *John Hawkesworth*, 159; Hawkesworth, *Account*.

53. Newell, *Trading Nature*, 145.

54. Hawkesworth, *Account*, 2:9.

55. Patel, *Explorations*, 270; Hawkesworth, *Account*, 1:462.

56. Patel, *Explorations*, 281; Hawkesworth, *Account*, 1:479.

57. Musgrave, *Multifarious Mr. Banks*, 174.

58. Patrick O'Brian, *Joseph Banks*, 151.

59. *Epistle from Oberea*.

60. Beaglehole, *The Endeavor Journal*, 279; Wilson, "Empire, Gender, and Modernity," 71–72.

61. Abbott, *John Hawkesworth*, 155–56, 167.

62. Wilson, "Empire, Gender, and Modernity," 40, 192; Hawkesworth, *Account*, 1:xvii.

63. Patel, *Explorations*, xx.

64. Dening, "Possessing Tahiti"; Wilson, "Empire, Gender and Modernity," 192.

2. 'Aimata

1. Henry, *Ancient Tahiti*, 249–50; Ellis, *Polynesian Researches*, 236–37.

2. Ellis, *London Missionary Society*, 239.

3. O'Reilly, *La vie à Tahiti*, 11–31, 221–26; Pritchard, *Queen Pomare*, 3–4; Davies, *Tahitian Mission*, 187. London Missionary Society missionary John Orsmond believed Pomare II's conversion to Christianity to be political: "The king changed his Gods, but he had no other reason but that of consolidating his Government." See Davies, *Tahitian Mission*, 350.

4. Pritchard, *Queen Pomare*, 6. For missionary journals and letters from the London Missionary Society's South Seas Mission, see South Seas Journals and Letters, 1796–1899, Inventory of Letters from Missionaries in Oceania (hereafter SSM), Special Collections and Archives, University of San Diego Library.

5. Stevenson, "'Aimata, Queen Pomare IV," 130.

6. Adams, *Tahiti*, 177; Stevenson, "'Aimata, Queen Pomare IV," 142n10.

7. Moerenhout, *Voyages aux îles*, 501.

8. Patty O'Brien, "'Think of Me,'" 111.

9. John Orsmond, journal, 1832–33, SSM.

10. Gunson, "Account," 228–30.

11. Newbury, *Tahiti Nui*, 47; Stevenson, "'Aimata, Queen Pomare IV," 142n9; Ellis, *London Missionary Society*, 239, 266.

12. Gunson, "Account," 230.

13. Gunson, "Account," 229–32.

14. Gunson, "Account," 231–32.

15. The missionary Henry Nott performed the marriage ceremony on December 3, 1832. See Gunson, "Account," 232–36; Newbury, *Tahiti Nui*, 61; Henry, *Ancient Tahiti*, 252.

16. Colin Newbury writes that the chiefs were more likely accusing 'Aimata of adultery in absence of an official divorce. See Newbury, *Tahiti Nui*, 60–61.

17. Gunson, "Account," 234.

18. Newell, *Trading Nature*, 178–83; Newbury, *Tahiti Nui*, 10.

19. Newell, *Trading Nature*, 178–83; Maud, "Tahitian Pork Trade," 209; Ellis, *London Missionary Society*, 129, 182.

20. Maude, "Tahitian Pork Trade," 211; Davies, *Tahitian Mission*, 192; Newbury, *Tahiti Nui*, 10.

21. Canning to Pomare, March 3, 1827, Records of the Foreign Office (as filmed by

the AJCP) / Pacific Island Correspondence / Vice-Counsel for Society Islands (hereafter FO), National Library of Australia.

22. Ellis, *London Missionary Society*, 290–91.

23. Ellis, *London Missionary Society*, 230; Davies, *Tahitian Mission*, 340–42.

24. Ellis, *London Missionary Society*, 321–27; Stevenson, "'Aimata, Queen Pomare IV,'" 134–35; Newbury, *Tahiti Nui*, 352.

25. Henry Nott, February 9, 1836, LMS.

26. Nott, *Evangelical Magazine*, 369–70, LMS; John Orsmond, journal, 1837, LMS.

27. Nott, February 9, 1836, LMS.

28. Nott, *Evangelical Magazine*, 371; Davies, *Tahitian Mission*, 359.

29. Pritchard had been seeking the office since 1832. See Patty O'Brien, "Think of Me," 113. Deckker discusses Pritchard's views on Catholic missionaries in Pritchard, *Aggressions*, 21–25.

30. O'Reilly, *La vie à Tahiti*, 221–26.

31. 'Aimata to Queen Victoria, January 20, 1841, LMS. See Simpson, *South Seas Journals and Letters*, SSM. See also Manktelow, *Gender, Power and Sexual Abuse*.

32. Pritchard, *Aggressions*, 40–45.

33. Two of the most complete chronological sources include Pritchard's *Aggressions* and Newbury's *Tahiti Nui*, although Pritchard writes from the perspective of 'Aimata and her English advisers.

34. Pritchard, *Aggressions*, 50–55; Stevenson, "'Aimata, Queen Pomare IV,'" 137; Patty O'Brien, "Think of Me," 114; Newell, *Trading Nature*, 212.

35. Pritchard had requested medical leave, but Deckker writes that Pritchard likely used the opportunity in England to press 'Aimata's case with the British Foreign Office. LaPlace arrived in 1841. The document was signed by Paraita, Paete, Hitorti, and Tati in June 1841. See Pritchard, *Aggressions*, 75–79. See also Newbury, "Resistance and Collaboration," 7.

36. Pōmare signed this document on September 9, 1842. See FO/58. See also Pritchard, *Aggressions*, 78–79, 91, 114–17.

37. Stevenson, "'Aimata, Queen Pomare IV,'" 140; Patty O'Brien, "Think of Me," 119.

38. Newbury, *Tahiti Nui*, 313n9; 'Aimata to Victoria, January 23, 1843, FO/58; 'Aimata to Victoria, November 8, 1838, FO/58; 'Aimata to Victoria, September 1, 1844, SSM.

39. 'Aimata to Victoria, January 22, 1843, FO/23.

40. 'Aimata to Louis-Philippe, November 9, 1843, FO/58.

41. 'Aimata to Louis-Philippe, September 25, 1844, SSM; Thomas Heath, April 27, SSM. See also Patty O'Brien, "Think of Me," 119.

42. 'Aimata, July 3, 1844, FO/58; Pritchard, *Aggressions*, 170, 188–89; Patty O'Brien, "Think of Me," 114.

43. Pritchard, *Queen Pomare*, 34–35.

44. Queen Victoria to King Leopold, October 17, August 27, and September 15, 1844, in Queen Victoria, *Letters of Queen Victoria*.

45. Queen Victoria, *Letters of Queen Victoria*, August 27, 1844; *Times* (London), March 29, 1843, FO/58.

46. 'Aimata to Victoria, November 10, 1843, LMS.

47. Manktelow, *Gender, Power and Sexual Abuse*, 175.

48. Newbury, *Tahiti Nui*, 56; Pritchard, *Queen Pomare*, 4; Lovitt, *London Missionary Society*, 230.

49. Patty O'Brien, "Think of Me," 112, 121; Pritchard, *Aggressions*, 56; Newbury, "Resistance and Collaboration," 15.

50. Pritchard, *Aggressions*, 130; George Platt, August 19, 1844, SSM; Newbury, "Resistance and Collaboration," 14–16.

51. Davies, *Tahitian Mission*, 358–59; Manktelow, *Gender, Power and Sexual Abuse*, 162.

52. Orsmond, July 30, 1845, LMS; Orsmond, journal, 1832–33, LMS.

53. Colonial Office to Foreign Office, August 1, 1839, FO/58; Palmerston to Pritchard, September 9, 1839, in Pritchard, *Aggressions*, 61.

54. Lord Aberdeen to Pritchard, September 25, 1843, FO/58; Orsmond, July 1845, LMS.

55. E. Buchanan, February 14, 1844, and Orsmond, July 1845, LMS.

56. Adams, *Tahiti*, 195; 'Aimata to George Charter, June 20, 1846, in Patty O'Brien, "Think of Me," 123.

57. G. Platt, January 9, 1844, LMS; O'Reilly, *La vie à Tahiti*, 11–31.

58. Stevenson, "'Aimata, Queen Pomare IV," 140.

59. Pomare to Pritchard, March 11, 1844, FO/58; and Alexander Salmon to Lord Aberdeen, November 8, 1843, FO/58.

60. Moerenhout, *Voyages aux îles*, 1:232–33; Pritchard, *Aggressions*, 196.

61. Henry, *Ancient Tahiti*, 249–50; John Orsmond, "Extracts from the Old Orsmond MS 1849," in Davies, *Tahitian Mission*, 253; 'Aimata, November 9, 1836, South Seas Journals, 1796–1899, Council for World Mission Archive, School of Oriental and African Studies Archives, University of London.

62. Henry, *Ancient Tahiti*, 249–50; Patty O'Brien, "Think of Me," 117. Moerenhout secured concessions in 1838 and again in 1842. See Pritchard, *Aggressions*, 45–50, 163; 'Aimata to Louis-Philippe, November 14, 1843, LMS.

63. Loti, *Marriage of Loti*, 115.

64. Olmstead, *Incidents of a Whaling Voyage*, 83.

65. Ellis, *London Missionary Society*, 404; Patty O'Brien, "Think of Me," 114.

66. Pōmare to Louis-Philippe, November 4, 1843, FO/20; Pōmare to Victoria, November 8, 1839, FO 58/15.

67. Adams, *Tahiti*, 177.

68. O'Reilly, *La vie à Tahiti*, 221–26.

3. Ka'ahumanu

1. See J. Cook, *Three Voyages*; and Vancouver, *Voyage of Discovery*. Cook's murder is discussed in detail by Marshal Sahlins in Sahlins, *Historical Metaphors*; and Sahlins, *How "Natives" Think*.
2. Vancouver, *Voyage of Discovery*, 5:95–96, 30, 87–88.
3. See Hackler, "Alliance or Cession?," 1–12.
4. Vancouver, *Voyage of Discovery*, 2:204–5.
5. Stokes, "New Bases for Hawaiian Chronology," 57, 60; Kamakau, *Ruling Chiefs of Hawaii*, 311.
6. Dibble, *History of the Sandwich Islands*, 193; Lorenzo Lyons, qtd. in Ralston, "Changes," 60; Emerson, "Address of the Retiring President," 38; W. D. Alexander, "Overthrow," 39; Bingham, *Residence*, 78; Russian explorer Otto von Kotzebue and Mercy Whitney, qtd. in Silverman, *Kaahumanu*, 57, 78.
7. Silverman, *Kaahumanu*, 31.
8. Kamakau, *Ruling Chiefs of Hawaii*, 175–78, 312–14.
9. Sahlins, *Historical Metaphors*, 56–58; Kamakau, *Ruling Chiefs of Hawaii*, 314–15.
10. Sahlins, *Historical Metaphors*, 54.
11. See Ralston, "Changes"; and D'Arcy, "Hawaiian Political Transformation," 85–108.
12. D'Arcy, "Hawaiian Political Transformation," 92. Keōpūolani often stayed indoors during the day for fear she would cause someone's death. See Sinclair, "Sacred Wife of Keōpūolani," 4; Kamakau, *Ruling Chiefs of Hawaii*, 224.
13. Valeri, *Kingship and Sacrifice*, 90–129.
14. Valerio, *Kingship and Sacrifice*, 90–129.
15. Ralston, "Changes," 51.
16. Ralston, "Changes," 51–52; Handy and Pukui, *Polynesian Family System*, 23–24.
17. Hackler, "Alliance or Cession," 5; D'Arcy, "Hawaiian Political Transformation," 94; Sahlins, *Historical Metaphors*, 54.
18. Dibble, *History of the Sandwich Islands*, 40–41, 91.
19. J. Cook, *Three Voyages*, 6:486; Rickman, *Journal*, 310–11.
20. J. Cook, *Three Voyages*, 7:11–2; Ralston, "Changes," 52–58.
21. Rickman, *Journal*, 289; Sahlins, *Historical Metaphors*, 47–48; Chappell, "Shipboard Relations," 147; W. D. Alexander, "Overthrow," 38.
22. Sahlins, *Historical Metaphors*, 55; Kame'eleihiwa, *Native Land*, 81. See Fish-Kashay, "From Kapus to Christianity," 17–39. Ka'ahumanu's infertility may have been the result of disease. By the 1850s only one in eleven Hawaiian women gave birth, and infant mortality hovered around 50 percent. See Igler, *Great Ocean*, 58.
23. Fish-Kashay, "From Kapus to Christianity," 28; Sahlins, *Historical Metaphors*, 63; Linnekin, *Sacred Queens*, 71; Kame'eleihiwa, *Native Land*, 73.
24. Silverman, *Kaahumanu*, 58; Kamakau, *Ruling Chiefs of Hawaii*, 220; W. D. Alexander, "Overthrow," 40.

25. Fish-Kashay, "From Kapus to Christianity," 26; Kameʻeleihiwa, *Native Land*, 81; Arago, *Narrative*, 88; L. Freycinet, *Hawaiʻi in 1819*, 19.

26. Linnekin, *Sacred Queens*, 71.

27. Sahlins, *Historical Metaphors*, 63; W. D. Alexander, "Overthrow," 39–40.

28. W. D. Alexander, "Overthrow," 41.

29. Rose de Freycinet, who was traveling with her husband, the captain of the *Uranie*, noted that William Pitt's wife stayed on the deck of the ship while her husband ate below because "she was tabooed." King Liholiho required Rose's husband to move huts after meeting with the king and his wives before the two men could drink wine. On the island of Hawaiʻi, the wife of a chief refused to eat pork, although she joined her husband for lunch aboard the ship. See R. Freycinet, *Woman of Courage*, 98, 101–2.

30. Dibble, *History of the Sandwich Islands*, 149–50; Kamakau, *Ruling Chiefs of Hawaii*, 225.

31. The source material regarding the timing of Makahiki is conflicting. Both Malo and Emerson agree that Kaʻahumanu planned for Liholiho to break ʻaikapu during Makahiki. Malo and Emerson write that Kaʻahumanu's feast occurred in ʻIkuwā (October). Yet Peter Corney, a foreigner traveling in the islands during 1817–20, wrote that Makahiki rituals had been shortened from four to two months: November (Welehu) and December (Makaliʻi). In different places Marshall Sahlins uses both October and November for the same feast. Malo and Kamakau record that the Kukahi rites for Makahiki originally occurred both in October (for the chiefs) and November (for the people). See Malo, *Hawaiian Antiquities*, 52–54; Emerson, "Address of the Retiring President," 38; Corney, *Voyages in the Northern Pacific*, 101–2; Sahlins, *Historical Metaphors*, 55, 65; Valeri, *Kingship and Sacrifice*, 200–203. W. D. Alexander, "Overthrow," 41–42. Don Francisco de Paula Marin, a Spanish resident on Oʻahu, noted in his journal that a ship arrived in Honolulu on November 6 with instructions from the king to end the ʻaikapu. The next day, November 7, "all the women ate pork, and they burnt all the [temples] on the island." This date would correspond with a November Kukahi feast. See Gast, *Don Francisco de Paula Marin*, 234.

32. W. D. Alexander, "Overthrow," 42; Valeri, *Kingship and Sacrifice*, 203–6; Ralston, "Changes," 54. Captain Cook's men may inadvertently have angered the Hawaiian people by using as firewood the piles of wooden gods that were in abeyance during Makahiki. See Sahlins, *How "Natives" Think*, 264–74.

33. Silverman, *Kaahumanu*, 69; W. D. Alexander, "Overthrow," 43; Bishop, *Missionary Herald*, 247.

34. *Missionary Herald*, qtd. in Thigpen, *Island Queens*, 52.

35. Bingham, *Residence*, 79.

36. Silverman, *Kaahumanu*, 89.

37. Vancouver, *Voyage of Discovery*, 5:93–94; Kamakau, *Ruling Chiefs of Hawaii*, 246–47; Silverman, *Kaahumanu*, 65; Arago, *Narrative*, 115.

38. Arago, *Narrative*, 108–11.

39. Sahlins, *Historical Metaphors*, 63; Kameʻeleihiwa, *Native Land*, 84–85.

40. Silverman, *Kaahumanu*, 92.

41. Silverman, *Kaahumanu*, 92.

42. Fish-Kashay, "From Kapus to Christianity," 35–36; Bingham, *Residence*, 214.

43. Kamakau, *Ruling Chiefs of Hawaii*, 319, 322–23; Bingham, *Residence*, 226; Silverman, *Kaahumanu*, 91–92; Sahlins, *Historical Metaphors*, 66; Stewart, *Residence*, 247–48.

44. Bingham, *Residence*, 260; Kamakau, *Ruling Chiefs of Hawaii*, 257, 275, 319; Silverman, *Kaahumanu*, 95.

45. Kamakau, *Ruling Chiefs of Hawaii*, 244, 254; Ellis, *Polynesian Researches*, 152.

46. Ellis, *Narrative of a Journal*, 39.

47. Kamakau, *Ruling Chiefs of Hawaii*, 223, 261; Ellis, *Memoir*, 132–33, 137; Silverman, *Kaahumanu*, 30.

48. Kamakau, *Ruling Chiefs of Hawaii*, 276, 284–85; Fish-Kashay, "Competing Imperialisms and Hawaiian Authority," 384; Silverman, *Kaahumanu*, 117; Ii, *Fragments of Hawaiian History*, 154–55; Arista, *Kingdom and the Republic*, 150, 180–94.

49. Kamakau, *Ruling Chiefs of Hawaii*, 323.

50. Auna, *Journal*, ABC 19.1 vol. 1, item 313, American Board of Commissioners for Foreign Missions Archives, Houghton Library, Harvard University.

51. Thigpen, *Island Queens*, 97.

52. Thigpen, *Island Queens*, 105–6; Grimshaw, "Missionary Wives," 43–44.

53. Bingham, *Residence*, 172; Linnekin, *Sacred Queens*, 72–73.

54. Hawaiian Constitutions of 1840, 1852, and 1864 in *Fundamental Law of Hawaii*.

55. R. Freycinet, *Woman of Courage*, 99; L. Freycinet, *Hawaiʻi in 1819*, 19, 23.

56. On Tahitian standards of beauty, see O'Reilly, *La vie à Tahiti*, 11–31. For insight into the attitudes of American missionary women, see Grimshaw, *Paths of Duty*, and Zwiep, *Pilgrim Path*.

57. French praise of Tahitian culture as being close to nature and, therefore, enlightened can be seen in Diderot, *Supplement to the Bougainville Voyage*.

4. Liliʻuokalani

1. The term *haole* originally meant "foreigner" and would not have applied to white persons born in the Hawaiian Islands such as the missionary children. However, due to the events of the nineteenth century, the word came to mean "white person," which is how it is used today. See Pukui and Elbert, *New Pocket Hawaiian Dictionary*.

2. Kaunui, *Paradoxes*, 124.

3. Kauanui, *Paradoxes*, 24.

4. *Statue Laws of His Majesty Kamehameha III*, 59.

5. Kauanui, *Paradoxes*, 136–37; Linnekin, *Sacred Queens*, 211–12; Liliuokalani, *Hawaii's Story*, 14.

6. Hobbs, *Hawaii*, 39–41; Kameʻeleihiwa, *Native Land*, 12. The Hawaiian legislature mandated cash payment of property taxes in 1846. See John Paris, qtd. in Linnekin, *Sacred Queens*, 197–98.

7. Linnekin, *Sacred Queens*, 217.

8. Ephraim Clark, qtd. in Grimshaw, "Missionary Wives," 35.

9. Grimshaw, "Missionary Wives," 43–44.

10. Recent scholarship suggests that the Hawaiian-language translation of "male subject" is gender neutral. However, Kauanui argues that English translations of the Hawaiian constitutions were given preference in practice. See Kauanui, *Paradoxes*, 147–49; Merry, *Colonizing Hawaiʻi*, 97; Osorio, *Dismembering Lāhui*, 45, 69; Silva, *Aloha Betrayed*, 43–44; Hawaiian Constitutions of 1840, 1852, and 1864 in *Fundamental Law of Hawaii*.

11. Kauanui, *Paradoxes*, 147–49; Liliʻuokalani, *Hawaii's Story*, 210.

12. Sadly, Prince Albert died at the age of four. Forbes, *In Haste with Aloha*, 3–6; Korn, "Queen Emma in France," 7.

13. Forbes, *In Haste with Aloha*, 6. On Kalākaua's reign, see Osorio, *Dismembering Lāhui*, 184, 199, 225, 287n121.

14. W. D. Alexander, *Later Years*, 11; Hawaiian Constitution of 1887 in *Fundamental Law of Hawaii*. Missionary descendants Lorrin Thurston, Sanford Dole, Sereno Bishop, Nathaniel Emerson, and William Castle were instrumental in forming the Hawaiian League, which eventually had over four hundred Honolulu members. The group organized a mass public meeting of Honolulu residents that passed resolutions demanding the king sign a new constitution under threat of force. See MacLennan, *Sovereign Sugar*, 235; and Osorio, *Dismembering Lāhui*, 235–38. For a partial list of attendees at the June 30, 1887, mass meeting, see *A Sketch of Recent Events Being a Short Account of the Events which Culminated on June 30, 1887, Together with a Full Report of the Great Reform Meeting, and the Two Constitutions in Parallel Columns* (Honolulu: A. M. Hewett, Hawaiian Gazette, 1887), Rare Manuscripts Division, Library of Congress.

15. Liliuokalani, *Hawaii's Story*, 209, 218–19.

16. Liliuokalani, *Diaries*, xxix–xxx.

17. Kuykendall, *Hawaiian Kingdom*, 581; W. D. Alexander, *Later Years*, 28.

18. Allen, *Betrayal of Liliuokalani*, 271–72.

19. Liliʻuokalani, *Hawaii's Story*, 274.

20. Kameʻeleihiwa, *Native Land*, 315; Liliʻuokalani, *Diaries*, 320. Daniel Dole was the first principal of Punahou School, which was originally established for missionary

children. The Dole family was distantly related to the later Doles of pineapple fame, who arrived in the islands much later. Lili'uokalani, *Diaries*, 471.

21. Allen, *Betrayal of Liliuokalani*, 288–89. David W. Forbes, who edited the published version of Lili'uokalani's diaries, calls Allen's biography "highly inaccurate" (xvi), and I concur. Allen's book, while heavily researched, contains inaccuracies and a lack of thorough citations. However, I find Allen's ideas regarding the Hawaiian art of chiefly negotiation interesting here, particularly in light of the fact that the queen's diary is silent between January 13 and January 17. At 9 a.m. on January 17, Lili'uokalani asked her *haole* friend Samuel Damon to come and "confer" with her "on the situation." At this point Damon had already been invited to join the provisional government. See Lili'uokalani, *Diaries*, 315–16. The revolutionaries could not understand why the queen did not attempt to thwart their activities or arrest them. In fact, on January 16, Lili'uokalani reiterated her commitment to constitutional mechanisms and avoiding bloodshed. Some interpreted her government's response as cowardice. See Dole, *Memoirs of the Hawaiian Revolution*, 79; Thurston, *Memoirs of the Hawaiian Revolution*, 256. See also Blount, *Affairs in Hawaii*, 213–14.

22. Lili'uokalani, *Hawaii's Story*, 420–22.

23. Lili'uokalani, *Hawaii's Story*, 422.

24. See Blount, *Affairs in Hawaii*; Dole, *Memoirs of the Hawaiian Revolution*, 113.

25. Grover Cleveland, "Message to Congress Regarding Hawaiian Annexation," December 18, 1893, Office of the Historian, Foreign Service Institute, United States Department of State, accessed November 20, 2022, https://history.state .gov/historicaldocuments/frus1894app2/pg_445.

26. Lili'uokalani, *Hawaii's Story*, 312.

27. Lili'uokalani, *Hawaii's Story*, 325–26.

28. L. K. Aholo, Oral History interview conducted by Helena G. Allen, 1969, Kamehameha Schools Archives.

29. Gulick and Gulick, *Pilgrims of Hawaii*, 309–11.

30. See, for example, "The Situation in Hawaii," *San Francisco Examiner*, March 6, 1893, 6; Walter G. Smith, "Suffrage in Hawaii: The Opinions of Sereno R. Bishop," *San Francisco Chronicle*, March 18, 1893, 3; "Sanguine Hawaii: Believe That Annexation Has Succeeded," *San Francisco Chronicle*, March 9, 1893, 1; Walter G. Smith, "Heathenism in Hawaii: Liliuokalani an Adept in its Practices," *San Francisco Chronicle*, March 13, 1893, 3; "Bedeviled Lili," *Brooklyn Daily Eagle*, February 9, 1893, 4; Sereno Bishop, Scrapbook, May 4, 189- and August 1900, Hawaiian Mission Children's Society; Kamehameha, *Evening Star* (Washington DC), April 21, 1894, 13; *Evening Star*, October 27, 1894, 13; *Evening Star*, July 7, 1897, 11; *Evening Star*, March 31, 1898, 11.

31. Lili'uokalani, *Diaries*, 202; Aholo, Oral History interview; Liliuokalani, *Hawaii's Story*, 317, 322, 372; Dole, *Memoirs of the Hawaiian Revolution*, 67.

32. Allen, *Betrayal of Liliuokalani*, 98, 162.

33. Lydia Bingham was recruited to lead the school in 1867. Her sister Elizabeth joined her in 1869. Both were the daughters of Hiram Bingham, who was a member of the first company of American missionaries who landed in the islands in 1820. See Bonura and Day, *American Girl*, xxvi.

34. Bonura and Day, *American Girl*, xxviii; Bonura, *Light*, 32.

35. Liliuokalani, *Hawaii's Story*, 139, 404. In 1880 missionary Laura Fish Judd wrote that only Scotland possessed a higher literacy rate. See Judd, *Sketches of Life*, 79.

36. Carol Chin has argued that Progressive Era American missionary women were beneficent imperialists: "As representatives of Christianity and American culture, the missionaries came to change, not to be changed." See Chin, "Beneficent Imperialists," 351.

37. Zackodnik, "Empire and Education," 158; Beyer, "Connection," 36–40, 44. Oberlin College's motto was "Learning and Labor." See "Oberlin History," Oberlin College and Conservatory, accessed September 26, 2019, www.oberlin.edu.

38. Oberlin's stated purpose was to "train teachers and other Christian leaders for the boundless most desolate fields in the West." See Waite, *Permission to Remain among Us*, 4, 96, 113.

39. Beyer, "Connection," 48; Bonura, *Light*, 23–24; Bonura and Day, *American Girl*, 20–22.

40. Bonura and Day, *American Girl*, xxvii, xxx, 23–24, 59; Bonura, *Light*, 59–61.

41. Chin, "Beneficent Imperialists," 351.

42. Carrie Winter, qtd. in Bonura and Day, *American Girl*, 16. Winter's letters to her fiancé and family are filled with examples of her and her fellow teachers' racism toward their Hawaiian students.

43. Winter, qtd. in Bonura and Day, *American Girl*, 139. On American teachers' mental and physical abuse of students, see 37, 56, 72–73.

44. Winter, qtd. in Bonura and Day, *American Girl*, 71. On Hawaiian geographic exploration, see Chang, *World*.

45. Lilla Appleton, qtd. in Bonura, *Light*, 117. On derision of the Hawaiian monarchy, see Bonura and Day, *American Girl*, 54, 286.

46. Student Lydia Aholo describes the school in an insightful student essay reprinted in Bonura and Day, *American Girl*, 41–44. On student resistance, see 168–69, 274, 278. On Christian mission, see xxx.

47. Hyde, qtd. in Bonura, *Light*, 35–36.

48. Winter, qtd. in Bonura and Day, *American Girl*, 234.

49. Trustee and missionary descendant William R. Castle published an article calling the queen "evil." Others published similar contempt. See Bonura, *Light*, 117, 126–28, 130–31.

50. Beyer, "Connection," 38–39, 45.

51. Allen, *Sanford Ballard Dole*, 186–87.

52. For the complicit role of white women in European colonialism, see Levine, "Introduction," 6–7.

53. Winter, qtd. in Bonura, *Light*, 86; Winter, qtd. in Bonura and Day, *American Girl*, 39, 259, 266.

54. *Course of Study for the Elementary Public Schools*, 15; *High School Course of Study*, 21; W. D. Alexander, *Brief History*, 314–15, 323.

55. *Biennial Report of the President*, 107; Amos Starr Cooke, "Communication to Teachers," June 1848, Hawaiian Mission Houses Archives, Honolulu, accessed October 15, 2019, www.missionhouses.org.

56. Liliʻuokalani only asked for half of the former Crown lands' valuation. See Allen, *Betrayal of Liliuokalani*, 370–73.

57. See Liliʻuokalani Trust, accessed February 10, 2021, https://onipaa.org/pages/the-trust. "He Inoa NōKaʻlulani" is a name song the queen composed after the birth of her niece. See Pukui, *Nā Wahine*, 26.

Conclusion

1. Aholo, Oral History interview; Liliuokalani, *Hawaii's Story*, 317, 322, 372.

2. Ellis, *London Missionary Society*, 6. See Dwight, *Memoirs of Henry Obookiah*; Kamakau, *Ruling Chiefs of Hawaii*, 246.

3. Igler, "Diseased Goods," 704.

4. Elisabeth Kaʻahumanu to Kamāmalu, August 1822, Aliʻi Letters, Hawaiian Evangelical Association Archives, 1853–1947, Hawaiian Mission Children's Society Library at the Hawaiian Mission Houses Historic Site and Archives, Honolulu.

5. Paraita to Cunningham, August 12, 1841, FO 58/16.

6. Aberdeen to Pritchard, September 25, 1843, FO 687/7.

7. Liliʻuokalani, *Hawaii's Story*, 389–91.

8. Liliʻuokalani, *Hawaii's Story*, 299, 302.

9. "Appeal to the Citizens," *Hawaiian Gazette*, January 17, 1893, 9; Pōmare, July 31, 1844, FO 58/27.

10. Bruat to Pōmare, January 31, 1844, FO 58/27.

11. Dole, *Memoirs of the Hawaiian Revolution*, 70–71.

12. Editorial, *Weekly Star*, February 16, 1853–April 20, 1853 (Box 3), Cooke Library Archives, Punahou School, Honolulu.

13. Porter, "North American Experience," 348–51; Ellis, *Memoir*, xii.

14. See Morrison, *Journal*. Tahitians were required to pay subscriptions to the London Missionary Society until 1848. See Newbury, *Tahiti Nui*, 124.

15. Bingham, *Residence*, 434; Allen, *Betrayal of Liliuokalani*, 40.

16. Wilhelm, "Meeting of 'Sister Sovereigns,'" 67.

17. Ledger-Lomas, *Queen Victoria*, 12; Liliʻuokalani, *Hawaii's Story*, 205.

18. Pritchard, *Aggressions*, 43–44, 53–54, 62–64; Kamakau, *Ruling Chiefs of Hawaii*, 331–32.

19. Shoemaker, *Pursuing Respect*, 7.

20. Salmond, *Aphrodite's Island*, 101–2.

21. 'Aimata to King Louis-Philippe, September 25, 1844, FO 58/26; 'Aimata to Queen Victoria, September 1, 1844, SSM.

22. British correspondence with the Hawaiian government and regarding 'Aimata's problems with France even can be found in the same folder. See FO 58/25.

23. Kamakau, *Ruling Chiefs of Hawaii*, 359–65; Liliuokalani, *Diaries*, 328.

24. *Times* (London), March 29, 1843, FO 58/20.

25. Lili'uokalani, *Diaries*, 335, 355, 382, 471; 'Aimata to Pritchard, March 11, 1844, LMS.

26. Gunson, *Messengers of Grace*, 25–26.

27. Porter, "North American Experience," 351.

28. Lili'uokalani, *Diaries*, 320, 470; Kaahumanu to Evarts, September 11, 1831, "Ali'i Letters," Hawaiian Mission Houses Digital Archive, accessed May 13, 2022, https://hmha.missionhouses.org/items/show/3021.

29. Lili'uokalani, *Hawaii's Story*, 397; John Addison Porter to Lili'uokalani, March 6, 1897, Bishop Museum Archives (BM), Honolulu; Lili'uokalani to McKinley, March 8, 1897, BM.

30. Lili'uokalani, *Diaries*, 468.

31. Lili'uokalani, *Diaries*, 473n20; Lili'uokalani, *Hawaii's Story*, 379–80, 404.

32. Miranda Johnson confirms this is true within British settler societies in Polynesia, including New Zealand. See Johnson, "Chiefly Women," 236–38. See also Burton, *Burdens of History*.

33. On gender and empire, see Rosenberg, "Gender," 116–24; Stoler, *Carnal Knowledge*; Rotter, "Gender Relations, Foreign Relations," 518–42; Bederman, *Manliness and Civilization*. On theory and morality-based foreign relations, see Nye, *Do Morals Matter?*; and McFarland et al., "Roundtable on Joseph S. Nye, Jr.," 13–24.

34. Public letters of support for 'Aimata and the London Missionary Society missionaries in Tahiti can be found in FO 58/22.

35. Lili'uokalani, *Diaries*, 471.

36. On U.S. empire, see Immerwahr, *How to Hide an Empire*. On citizenship and race, see Gabaccia, *Foreign Relations*. On trade protectionism, see MacLennan, *Sovereign Sugar*. Anti-imperialists included those who saw "racial uplift" as a national priority and way to achieve full employment. See Anderson, "Northern Foundations," 287–312.

37. Liliuokalani, *Hawaii's Story*, 407.

Bibliography

Archives and Manuscript Materials

American Board of Commissioners for Foreign Missions Archives, Houghton Library, Harvard University, Cambridge MA.

Bishop Museum Archives, Honolulu HI.

Cooke Library Archives, Punahou School, Honolulu HI.

Foreign Office records, 1761–1952 [microform] (as filmed by the Australia Joint Copying Project [AJCP]), National Library of Australia.

Hawaiian Evangelical Association Archives, 1853–1947, Hawaiian Mission Children's Society Library at the Hawaiian Mission Houses Historic Site and Archives, Honolulu HI.

Kamehameha Schools Archives, Honolulu HI.

London Missionary Society's South Seas Mission, South Seas Journals and Letters, 1796–1899, Inventory of Letters from Missionaries in Oceania, Special Collections and Archives, University of San Diego Library.

Rare Manuscripts Division, Library of Congress, Washington DC.

Records of the London Missionary Society (as filmed by the AJCP), Series, Letters from missionaries in the Society and Hervey Islands and also the Marquesas, Samoan and Sandwich Islands, 1835–1836, National Library of Australia.

Research and Collections, State Library of New South Wales, Australia.

South Seas Journals, 1796–1899, Council for World Mission Archive, School of Oriental and African Studies Archives, University of London.

Published Works

Abbott, John Lawrence. *John Hawkesworth: Eighteenth-Century Man of Letters.* Madison: University of Wisconsin Press, 1982.

Adams, Henry. *Tahiti: Memoirs of Marau Taaroa, Last Queen of Tahiti.* New York: Scholar's Facsimiles and Reprints, 1947.

Alexander, Caroline. *The Bounty: The True Story of the Mutiny on the Bounty.* New York: Penguin, 2003.

Alexander, W. D. *A Brief History of the Hawaiian People*. New York: American Book, 1899.

———. *History of Later Years of the Hawaiian Monarchy and the Revolution of 1893*. Honolulu: Hawaiian Gazette, 1896.

———. "Overthrow of the Ancient Tabu System in the Hawaiian Islands." In *Twenty-Fifth Annual Report of the Hawaiian Historical Society for the Year 1916*, 37–45. Honolulu: Paradise of the Pacific Press, 1917.

Allen, Helena G. *The Betrayal of Liliuokalani: Last Queen of Hawaii, 1838–1917*. Honolulu: Mutual, 1982.

———. *Sanford Ballard Dole: Hawaii's Only President, 1844–1926*. Glendale CA: Arthur H. Clark, 1988.

Anderson, James D. "Northern Foundations and the Shaping of Southern Black Rural Education, 1902–1935." In *The Social History of American Education*, edited by B. Edward McClellan and William J. Reese, 287–312. Urbana: University of Illinois Press, 1988.

Andrew, John A., III. *Rebuilding the Christian Commonwealth: New England Congregationalists and Foreign Missions, 1800–1830*. Lexington: University Press of Kentucky, 1976.

Arago, J. *Narrative of a Voyage round the World in the* Uranie *and* Physicienne *Corvettes, Commanded by Captain Freycinet*. London: Treuttel and Wurtz, 1823.

Arista, Neolani. *The Kingdom and the Republic: Sovereign Hawai'i and the Early United States*. Philadelphia: University of Pennsylvania Press, 2019.

Beaglehole, J. C. *The Endeavor Journal of Joseph Banks, 1768–1771*. Sydney: Halstead Press, 1962.

Bederman, Gail. *Manliness and Civilization: A Cultural History of Gender and Race in the United States, 1880–1917*. Chicago: University of Chicago Press, 1996.

Beyer, Kalani. "The Connection of Samuel Chapman Armstrong as Both Borrower and Architect of Education in Hawai'i." *History of Education Quarterly* 47, no. 1 (2007): 23–48.

Biennial Report of the President of the Board of Education to the Legislature of the Republic of Hawaii, 1896. Honolulu: Hawaiian Gazette, 1896.

Bingham, Hiram. *A Residence of Twenty-One Years in the Sandwich Islands*. Hartford CT: Hezekiah Huntington, 1848.

Bishop, Artemis. *Missionary Herald* 23 (1827): 246–47.

Blount, James. *Affairs in Hawaii*. Washington DC: U.S. Government Printing Office, 1895.

Bonura, Sandra E. *Light in the Queen's Garden: Ida May Pope, Pioneer for Hawai'i's Daughters, 1862–1914*. Honolulu: University of Hawai'i Press, 2017.

Bonura, Sandra E., and Deborah Day. *An American Girl in the Hawai'ian Islands: Letters of Carrie Prudence Winter, 1890–1893*. Honolulu: University of Hawai'i Press, 2012.

Burton, Antoinette. *Burdens of History: British Feminists, Indian Women, and Imperial Culture, 1865–1915*. Chapel Hill: University of North Carolina Press, 1994.

Carey, Hilary M. "Companions in the Wilderness? Missionary Wives in Colonial Australia, 1788–1900." *Journal of Religious History* 19, no. 2 (December 1995): 227–48.

Carrington, Hugh. *The Discovery of Tahiti: A Journal of the Second Voyage of H.M.S. Dolphin round the World, under the Command of Captain Wallis, R.N.: In the Years 1766, 1767, and 1768, Written by Her Master, George Robertson*. London: Hakluyt Society, 1948.

Chang, David A. *The World and All the Things upon It: Native Hawaiian Geographies of Exploration*. Minneapolis: University of Minnesota Press, 2016.

Chappell, David. "Shipboard Relations between Pacific Island Women and Euroamerican Men, 1767–1887." *Journal of Pacific History* 27 (December 1992): 131–49.

Chernock, Arianne. *The Right to Rule and the Rights of Women: Queen Victoria and the Women's Movement*. Cambridge: Cambridge University Press, 2019.

Chin, Carol C. "Beneficent Imperialists: American Women Missionaries in China at the Turn of the Twentieth Century." *Diplomatic History* 27, no. 3 (June 2003): 327–52.

Coloma, Roland Sintos. "'Destiny Has Thrown the Negro and the Filipino under the Tutelage of America': Race and Curriculum in the Age of Empire." *Ontario Institute for Studies in Education* 39, no. 4 (2009): 496–519.

Conroy-Krutz, Emily. *Christian Imperialism: Converting the World in the Early American Republic*. Ithaca NY: Cornell University Press, 2018.

Cook, James. *The Journals of Captain Cook*. Edited by Philip Edwards. London: Penguin, 1999.

———. *The Three Voyages of Captain James Cook round the World*. 7 vols. London: Longman, Hurst, Rees, Orme, and Brown, 1821.

Cook, Kealani. *Return to Kahiki: Native Hawaiians in Oceania*. Cambridge: Cambridge University Press, 2018.

Corney, Peter. *Voyages in the Northern Pacific*. Honolulu: Thos. G. Thrum, 1896.

Cott, Nancy F. *The Bonds of Womanhood: "Woman's Sphere" in New England, 1780–1835*. New Haven CT: Yale University Press, 1977.

Course of Study for the Elementary Public Schools of Hawaii. Honolulu: Hawaiian Gazette, 1899.

D'Arcy, Paul. "The Hawaiian Political Transformation from 1770 to 1796." In *Transforming Hawai'i: Balancing Coercion and Consent in Eighteenth-Century Kānaka Maoli Statecraft*, 85–108. Australia: ANU Press, 2018.

Davies, John. *The History of the Tahitian Mission: 199–1830*. Edited by C. W. Newbury. Cambridge: Cambridge University Press, 1961.

Demuth, Bathsheba. *Floating Coast: An Environmental History of the Bering Strait*. New York: W. W. Norton, 2019.

Dening, Greg. "Possessing Tahiti." *Archaeology in Oceania* 21, no. 1 (April 1986): 103–18.

Dibble, Sheldon. *History of the Sandwich Islands*. Lahainaluna: Press of the Mission Seminary, 1843.

Diderot, Denis. *Supplement to the Bougainville Voyage*. Paris: Larousse, 1796.

Dole, Sanford Ballard. *Memoirs of the Hawaiian Revolution*. Edited by Andrew Farrell. Honolulu: Advertiser, 1936.

Druett, Joan. *Tupaia: Captain Cook's Polynesian Navigator*. Santa Barbara CA: Praeger, 2011.

Dwight, Edwin Welles. *Memoirs of Henry Obookiah: A Native of Owhyhee, and a Member of the Foreign Mission School; Who Died at Cornwall, Conn. Feb. 17, 1818 Aged 26 Years*. Philadelphia: American Sunday School Union, 1830.

Eittreim, Elisabeth M. *Teaching Empire: Native Americans, Filipinos, and U.S. Imperial Education, 1879–1918*. Lawrence: University Press of Kansas, 2019.

Ellis, William. *The History of the London Missionary Society*. London: John Snow, 1844.

———. *Memoir of Mrs. Mary Mercy Ellis*. Boston: Crocker & Brewster, 1836.

———. *A Narrative of a Journal through Hawaii*. Honolulu: Hawaiian Gazette, 1917.

———. *Polynesian Researches during a Residence of Nearly Six Years in the South Seas Islands*. London: Fisher, Son, and Jackson, 1829.

Emerson, N. B. "Address of the Retiring President N. B. Emerson, M.D.: Cause of Decline of Ancient Hawaiian Sports." In *Fortieth Annual Report of the Hawaiian Mission Children's Society*, 33–44. Honolulu: Press Publishing, 1892.

An Epistle from Oberea, Queen of Otaheite, to Joseph Banks, Esq., Translated by T.Q.Z. Esq., Professor of the Otaheite Language in Dublin, and of all the Language of the Undiscovered Islands in the South Sea. 4th ed. London: J. Almon, 1774.

Fara, Patricia. *Sex, Botany, & Empire: The Story of Carl Linnaeus and Joseph Banks*. London: Icon Books, 2003.

Fish-Kashay, Jennifer. "Competing Imperialisms and Hawaiian Authority: The Cannonading of Lāhainā in 1827." *Pacific Historical Review* 77, no. 3 (August 2008): 369–90.

———. "From Kapus to Christianity: The Disestablishment of the Hawaiian Religion and Chiefly Appropriation of Calvinist Christianity." *Western Historical Quarterly* 39, no. 1 (Spring 2008): 17–39.

Forbes, David W. *In Haste with Aloha: Letters and Diaries of Queen Emma, 1881–1885*. Honolulu: University of Hawai'i Press, 2017.

Freycinet, Louis Claude de Saulses de. *Hawai'i in 1819: A Narrative Account*. Translated by Ella L. Wiswell. Honolulu: Bishop Museum, 1978.

Freycinet, Rose de. *A Woman of Courage: The Journal of Rose de Freycinet on Her Voyage around the World, 1817–1820*. Translated and edited by Marc Sere Rivière. Canberra: National Library of Australia, 1996.

Fulton, Richard, Stephen Hancock, Peter Hoffenberg, and Allison Paynter, eds. *South Seas Encounters: Nineteenth-Century Oceania, Britain, and America*. New York: Routledge, 2018.

Fundamental Law of Hawaii. Edited by Lorrin A. Thurston. Honolulu: Hawaiian Gazette, 1904.

Gabaccia, Donna R. *Foreign Relations: American Immigration in Global Perspective*. Princeton NJ: Princeton University Press, 2012.

Gast, Ross H. *Don Francisco de Paula Marin: A Biography and the Letters and Journals of Francisco de Paula Marin*. Edited by Agnes C. Conrad. Honolulu: University Press of Hawai'i, 1973.

Grimshaw, Patricia. "New England Missionary Wives, Hawaiian Women and 'The Cult of True Womanhood.'" In Jolly and Macintyre, *Family and Gender*, 19–44.

———. *Paths of Duty: American Missionary Wives in Nineteenth-Century Hawaii*. Honolulu: University of Hawai'i Press, 1989.

Gulick, Orramel Hinckley, and Ann Eliza Clark Gulick. *The Pilgrims of Hawaii: Their Own Story of Their Pilgrimage from New England and Life Work in the Sandwich Islands, Now Known as Hawaii; with Explanatory and Illustrative Material Compiled and Verified from Original Sources*. New York: Fleming H. Revell, 1918.

Gunson, Niel. "An Account of the Mamaia or Visionary Heresy of Tahiti, 1826–1841." *Journal of the Polynesian Society* 71, no. 2 (June 1962): 209–43.

———. "Great Women and Friendship Contract Rites in Pre-Christian Tahiti." *Journal of the Polynesian Society* 73, no. 1 (March 1964): 53–69.

———. *Messengers of Grace: Evangelical Missionaries in the South Seas, 1797–1860*. Melbourne: Oxford University Press, 1978.

———. "Sacred Women Chiefs and Female 'Headmen' in Polynesian History." *Journal of Pacific History* 22, no. 3 (July 1987): 139–72.

Hackler, Rhoda E. A. "Alliance or Cession? Missing Letter from Kamehameha I to King George III of England Casts Light on 1794 Agreement." *Hawaiian Journal of History* 20 (1986): 1–12.

Handy, E. S. Craighill, and Mary Kawena Pukui. *The Polynesian Family System in Ka'u, Hawai'i*. Honolulu: Mutual, 1998.

Hardwick, Julie. "Fractured Domesticity in the Old Regine: Families and Global Goods in Eighteenth-Century France." *American Historical Review* 124, no. 4 (October 2019): 1267–77.

Haskins, Victoria. "Domesticating Colonizers: Domesticity, Indigenous Domestic Labor, and the Modern Settler Colonial Nation." *American Historical Review* 124, no. 4 (October 2019): 1290–301.

Hawkesworth, John. *An Account of the Voyages Undertaken by the Order of His Present Majesty for Making Discoveries in the Southern Hemisphere, and Successively Performed by Commodore Byron, Captain Carteret, Captain Wallis, and Captain Cook, in the Dolphin, the Swallow, and the Endeavor: Drawn Up from the Journals which were Kept by the Several Commanders, and from the Papers of Joseph Banks, Esq. in Three Volumes*. London: Strahan and Cadell, 1773.

Henry, Teuira. *Ancient Tahiti*. Honolulu: Bernice P. Bishop Museum, 1928.

Herbert, Christopher. *Gold Rush Manliness: Race and Gender on the Pacific Slope*. Seattle: University of Washington Press, 2018.

High School Course of Study, Part 2, Section VI Social Science. Territory of Hawaii: Department of Public Instruction, 1927.

Hobbs, Jean, *Hawaii: A Pageant of the Soil*. Stanford CA: Stanford University Press, 1935.

Hoganson, Kristin L. *Fighting for American Manhood: How Gender Politics Provoked the Spanish-American and Philippine-American Wars*. New Haven CT: Yale University Press, 1998.

Hunter, Jane. *The Gospel of Gentility: American Women Missionaries in Turn-of-the-Century China*. New Haven CT: Yale University Press, 1984.

Igler, David. "Diseased Goods: Global Exchanges in the Eastern Pacific Basin, 1770–1850." *American Historical Review* 109, no. 3 (June 2004): 693–719.

———. *The Great Ocean: Pacific Worlds from Captain Cook to the Gold Rush*. Oxford: Oxford University Press, 2013.

Ii, John Papa. *Fragments of Hawaiian History*. Honolulu: Bishop Museum Press, 1959.

Immerwahr, Daniel. *How to Hide an Empire: A History of the Greater United States*. New York: Picador, 2019.

Jacobs, Margaret. *White Mother to a Dark Race: Settler Colonialism, Maternalism, and the Removal of Indigenous Children in the American West and Australia, 1880–1940*. Lincoln: University of Nebraska Press, 2011.

Johnson, Miranda. "Chiefly Women: Queen Victoria, Meri Mangakahia, and the Māori Parliament." In *Mistress of Everything: Queen Victoria in Indigenous Worlds*, edited by Sarah Carter and Maria Nugent, 228–45. Manchester: Manchester University Press, 2016.

Jolly, Margaret, and Martha Macintyre, eds. *Family and Gender in the Pacific*. New York: Cambridge University Press, 1989.

Judd, Laura Fish. *Sketches of Life in the Hawaiian Islands: 1828–1861*. New York: Anson D. F. Randolph, 1880.

Kamakau, Samuel. *Ruling Chiefs of Hawaii*. Honolulu: Kamehameha Schools Press, 1961.

Kameʻeleihiwa, Lilikalā. *Native Land and Foreign Desires: Pehea Lā E Pono Ai?* Honolulu: Bishop Museum Press, 1992.

Kauanui, J. Kehaulani. *Paradoxes of Hawaiian Sovereignty: Land, Sex, and the Colonial Politics of State Nationalism*. Durham NC: Duke University Press, 2018.

Korn, A. L. "Queen Emma in France: 1865–6." In *Sixty-Fifth Annual Report of the Hawaiian Historical Society for the Year 1956*, 7–24. Honolulu: Advertiser, 1957.

Kuykendall, Ralph S. *The Hawaiian Kingdom, 1874–1893: The Kalakaua Dynasty*. Vol. 3. Honolulu: University of Hawaiʻi Press, 1967.

Ledger-Lomas, Michael. *Queen Victoria: This Thorny Crown*. Oxford: Oxford University Press, 2021.

Levine, Philippa. "Introduction: Why Gender and Empire." In *Gender and Empire*, edited by Philippa Levine, 1–13. Oxford: Oxford University Press, 2004.

Lew-Williams, Beth. *The Chinese Must Go: Violence, Exclusion, and the Making of the Alien in America*. Cambridge MA: Harvard University Press, 2018.

Liliuokalani. *The Diaries of Queen Liliuokalani of Hawaii: 1885–1900*. Edited and annotated by David W. Forbes. Honolulu: Hui Hānai, 2019.

———. *Hawaii's Story by Hawaii's Queen*. Honolulu: Hui Hānai, 2013.

Linnekin, Jocelyn. *Sacred Queens and Women of Consequence: Rank, Gender, and Colonialism in the Hawaiian Islands*. Ann Arbor: University of Michigan Press, 1990.

Loti, Pierre. *The Marriage of Loti*. Translated by Clara Hill. London: T. Werner Laurie, 1880.

Lovitt, Richard. *The History of the London Missionary Society: 1795–1895*. Oxford: Oxford University Press, 1899.

MacLennan, Carol A. *Sovereign Sugar: Industry and Environment in Hawai'i*. Honolulu: University of Hawai'i Press, 2014.

Madley, Benjamin. *American Genocide: The United States and the California Indian Tragedy*. New Haven CT: Yale University Press, 2017.

Malo, David. *Hawaiian Antiquities (Moolelo Hawaii)*. Honolulu: Hawaiian Gazette, 1898.

Manktelow, Emily J. *Gender, Power and Sexual Abuse in the Pacific: Rev. Simpson's "Improper Liberties."* London: Bloomsbury, 2018.

Matsuda, Matt K. *Pacific Worlds: A History of Seas, Peoples, and Cultures*. Cambridge: Cambridge University Press, 2012.

Maud, H. E. "The Tahitian Pork Trade: 1800–1830: An Episode in Australia's Commercial History." In *Of Islands and Men: Studies in Pacific History*. Melbourne: Oxford University Press, 1968.

McFarland, Kelly M., Lori Clune & Danielle Richman, Wilson D. (Billy) Misamble, C.S.C., Seth Jacobs, Vanessa Walker, and Joseph S. Nye Jr. "A Roundtable on Joseph S. Nye, Jr., *Do Morals Matter?: Presidents and Foreign Policy from FDR to Trump*." Passport: *The Society for Historians of American Foreign Relations Review* 51, no. 2. (September 2020): 13–24.

Melillo, Edward D. "Making Sea Cucumbers out of Whales' Teeth: Nantucket Castaways and Encounters of Value in Nineteenth-Century Fiji." *Environmental History* 20, no. 3. (July 2015): 449–74.

Merry, Sally Engle. *Colonizing Hawai'i: The Cultural Power of the Law*. Princeton NJ: Princeton University Press, 2000.

Moerenhout, J. A. *Voyages aux îles du Grand océan*. 2 vols. Paris: A. Bertrand, 1837.

Morgan, Philip D. "Encounters between British and 'Indigenous' Peoples, c. 1500–c. 1800." In *Empire and Others: British Encounters with Indigenous Peoples, 1600–1850*, edited by Martin Daunton and Rick Halpern, 42–78. Philadelphia, University of Pennsylvania Press, 1999.

Musgrave, Toby. *The Multifarious Mr. Banks: From Botany Bay to Kew, the Natural Historian Who Shaped the World.* New Haven CT: Yale University Press, 2020.

Newbury, Colin. "Resistance and Collaboration in French Polynesia: The Tahitian War: 1844–7." *Journal of the Polynesian Society* 82, no. 1 (March 1973): 5–27.

———. *Tahiti Nui: Change and Survival in French Polynesia, 1767–1945.* Honolulu: University of Hawai'i Press, 1980.

Newell, Jennifer. *Trading Nature: Tahitians, Europeans & Ecological Exchange.* Honolulu: University of Hawai'i Press, 2010.

Nott, Henry. *The Evangelical Magazine and Missionary Chronicle* 14 (August 1836): 369–71.

Nye, Joseph S., Jr. *Do Morals Matter? Presidents and Foreign Policy from FDR to Trump.* New York: Oxford University Press, 2020.

O'Brian, Patrick. *Joseph Banks: A Life.* Chicago: University of Chicago Press, 1987.

O'Brien, Patty. "'Think of Me as a Woman': Queen Pomare of Tahiti and Anglo-French Imperial Contest in the 1840s Pacific." *Gender and History* 18, no. 1 (April 2006): 108–29.

Oliver, Douglas L. *Ancient Tahitian Society.* Honolulu: University Press of Hawai'i, 1974.

Olmstead, Francis Allyn. *Incidents of a Whaling Voyage.* New York: D. Appleton, 1841.

O'Reilly, Patrick. *La vie à Tahiti au temps de la reine Pomaré.* Paris: Société des Océanistes, 1975.

Osorio, Jonathan Kay Kamakawiwo'ole. *Dismembering Lāhui: A History of the Hawaiian Nation to 1887.* Honolulu: University of Hawai'i Press, 2002.

Pascoe, Peggy. *Relations of Rescue: The Search for Female Moral Authority in the American West, 1874–1939.* New York: Oxford University Press, 1993.

Patel, Sandhya. *Exploration of the South Seas in the Eighteenth Century: Rediscovered Accounts.* Vol. 1, *Samuel Wallis's Voyage round the World in the Dolphin, 1766–1768.* London: Routledge, 2016.

Perry, Adele. "From 'the Hot-Bed of Vice' to the 'Good and Well-Ordered Christian Home': First Nations Housing and Reform in Nineteenth-Century British Columbia." *Ethnohistory: The Bulletin of the Ohio Valley Historic Indian Conference* 50, no. 4 (2003): 587–610.

Porter, Andrew. "North American Experience and British Missionary Encounters in Africa and the Pacific, c. 1800–50." In *Empire and Others: British Encounters with Indigenous Peoples, 1600–1850,* edited by Marti Daunton and Rick Halpern, 345–63. Philadelphia: University of Pennsylvania Press, 1999.

Porterfield, Amanda. *Mary Lyon and the Mount Holyoke Missionaries.* New York: Oxford University Press, 1997.

Pritchard, George. *The Aggressions of the French at Tahiti and Other Islands in the Pacific.* Edited by Paul de Deckker. Auckland: Auckland University Press, 1983.

———. *Queen Pomare and Her Country.* London: Elliott Stock, 1879.

Pukui, Mary Kawena. *Nā Wahine: Hawaiian Proverbs and Inspirational Quotes Celebrating Women in Hawai'i.* Honolulu: Mutual, 2002.

Pukui, Mary Kawena, and Samuel H. Elbert. *New Pocket Hawaiian Dictionary.* Honolulu: University of Hawai'i Press, 1975.

Ralston, Caroline. "Changes in the Ordinary Lives of Ordinary Women in Early Post-Colonial Hawaii." In Jolly and Macintyre, *Family and Gender,* 45–64.

Ravalli, Richard. *Sea Otters: A History.* Lincoln: University of Nebraska Press, 2018.

Reeves-Ellington, Barbara. "Women, Protestant Missions, and American Cultural Expansion, 1800 to 1938: A Historiographical Sketch." *Social Sciences and Missions* 24 (2011): 1–16.

Rickman, John. *Journal of Captain Cook's Last Voyage to the Pacific Ocean on Discovery.* London: E. Newbury, 1781.

Rosenberg, Emily S. "Gender." *Journal of American History* 77 (June 1990): 116–24.

———. *Spreading the American Dream: American Economic and Cultural Expansion, 1890–1945.* New York: Hill and Wang, 1982.

Rotter, Andrew. "Gender Relations, Foreign Relations: The United States and South Asia, 1947–1964." *Journal of American History* 81, no. 2 (September 1994): 518–42.

Sahlins, Marshall. *Historical Metaphors and Mythical Realities.* Ann Arbor: University of Michigan Press, 1981.

———. *How "Natives" Think: About Captain Cook, for Example.* Chicago: University of Chicago Press, 1995.

Salmond, Anne. *Aphrodite's Island: The European Discovery of Tahiti.* Berkeley: University of California Press, 2009.

Schulz, Joy. *Hawaiian by Birth: Missionary Children, Bicultural Identity, and U.S. Colonialism in the Pacific.* Lincoln: University of Nebraska Press, 2017.

Scott, Anne Firor. "The Ever-Widening Circle: The Diffusion of Feminist Values from the Troy Female Seminary, 1822–1872." In *The Social History of American Education,* edited by B. Edward McClellan and William J. Reese. Urbana: University of Illinois Press, 1988.

Shoemaker, Nancy. *Pursuing Respect in the Cannibal Isles: Americans in Nineteenth-Century Fiji.* Ithaca NY: Cornell University Press, 2018.

Silva, Noenoe K. *Aloha Betrayed: Native Hawaiian Resistance to American Colonialism.* Durham NC: Duke University Press, 2004.

———. "Mana Hawai'i: An Examination of Political Uses of the Word Mana in Hawaiian." In *New Mana: Transformations of a Classic Concept in Pacific Languages and Cultures,* edited by Matt Tomlinson and Ty P. Kāwika Tengan, 37–54. Canberra: Australian National University Press, 2016.

Silverman, Jane L. *Kaahumanu: Molder of Change*. Honolulu: Friends of the Judiciary History Center of Hawaii, 1987.

Sinclair, Marjorie. "The Sacred Wife of Keōpūolani." *Hawaiian Journal of History* 5 (1971): 3–23.

Smith, Jewel A. *Transforming Women's Education: Liberal Arts and Music in Female Seminaries*. Urbana: University of Illinois Press, 2019.

Statue Laws of His Majesty Kamehameha III, A.D. 1845 and 1846. Honolulu: Charles E. Hitchcock, 1846.

Stevenson, Karen. "'Aimata, Queen Pomare IV: Thwarting Adversity in Early 19th Century Tahiti." *Journal of the Polynesian Society* 123, no. 2 (June 2014): 129–44.

Stewart, C. S. *A Residence in the Sandwich Islands*. Boston: Weeks, Jordan, 1839.

Stokes, John F. G. "New Bases for Hawaiian Chronology." In *Forty-First Annual Report of the Hawaiian Historical Society for the Year 1932*, 23–65. Honolulu: Print Shop, 1933.

Stoler, Ann Laura. *Carnal Knowledge and Imperial Power: Race and the Intimate in Colonial Rule*. Berkeley: University of California Press, 2002.

Thigpen, Jennifer. *Island Queens and Mission Wives: How Gender and Empire Remade Hawai'i's Pacific World*. Chapel Hill: University of North Carolina Press, 2014.

Thurston, Lorrin A. *Memoirs of the Hawaiian Revolution*. Edited by Andrew Farrell. Honolulu: Advertiser, 1936.

Tyrrell, Ian. *Reforming the World: The Creation of America's Moral Empire*. Princeton NJ: Princeton University Press, 2010.

Valeri, Valerio. *Kingship and Sacrifice: Ritual and Society in Ancient Hawaii*. Chicago: University of Chicago Press, 1985.

Vancouver, George. *A Voyage of Discovery to the North Pacific Ocean and round the World*. 6 vols. London: John Stockdale, 1801.

Victoria, Queen. *The Letters of Queen Victoria*. Vol. 2, *1844–1853*. Edited by Arthur Christopher Benson and Viscount Esher. London: J. Murray, 1907. Project Gutenberg eBook, 2008.

Waite, Cally L. *Permission to Remain among Us: Education for Blacks in Oberlin, Ohio, 1880–1914*. Westport CT: Praeger, 2002.

Welter, Barbara. "The Cult of True Womanhood: 1820–1860." *American Quarterly* 18, no. 2, part 1 (Summer 1966).

Wilhelm, Lindsay Puawehiwa. "A Meeting of 'Sister Sovereigns': Hawaiian Royalty at Victoria's Golden Jubilee." In Fulton et al., *South Seas Encounters*, 63–86.

Wilson, Kathleen. "Empire, Gender, and Modernity in the Eighteenth Century." In *Gender and Empire*, edited by Philippa Levine, 14–45. Oxford: Oxford University Press, 2007.

Yokota, Kariann Akemi. *Unbecoming British: How Revolutionary America Became a Postcolonial Nation*. Oxford: Oxford University Press, 2011.

Zackodnik, Teresa. "Empire and Education in Hampton's Southern Workman: The South Pacific, the Caribbean and the Reconstruction South." In Fulton et al., *South Seas Encounters*, 156–74.

Zwiep, Mary. *Pilgrim Path: The First Company of Women Missionaries to Hawaii.* Madison: University of Wisconsin Press, 1991.

Index

Page numbers in italics refer to illustrations.

Haweis, Thomas, 96
Hawkesworth, John, 28–31, 35, 96
Heath, Thomas, 46
hierarchal systems, 16–17
Hina, 5
HMS *Bounty*, 29, 40
HMS *Discovery*, 59
HMS *Dolphin*, 1, 19–30
HMS *Endeavor*, 1, 28, 63
HMS *Resolution*, 62
HMS *Venus*, 40
Homestead Act (1862), 9
homosexuality, 10
Hoʻohōkūkalani, 5
House of Nobles, 79–80, 82
Huahine, 4
humility, 82
Hyde, Charles, 90

Igler, David, 26
immigration laws, 41
industrial vs. intellectual labor, 9–10
infanticide, 17
infant mortality, 121n22
infectious diseases, 26, 62, 63, 96. *See also* prostitution
infertility, 58, 121n22
informal empire as concept, 8
island geography and genealogies, 4–6

John Palmer (ship), 72
Judd, Gerrit, 78, 102

Kaʻahumanu (1768–1832), 60, *71*, *75*; on British arrival, 1; infertility of, 58, 121n22; *palapala* by, 96–97; as political leader, 58–59, 64–65, 68, 72–75, 77; religion and, 63–70, 102
Kaahumanu Society, 86–87
kahiki as term, 5. *See also* Tahiti

kahuna, 60, 81
Kaʻiulani, 93
Kālaimoku, 68
Kalākaua, David, 81–82, 87, 90, 99
Kamakaʻeha, Liliʻu Loloku Walania. *See* Liliʻuokalani (1839–1917)
Kamakau, Samuel, 10, 58, 59, 69, 70
Kamāmalu, 69
Kameʻeleihiwa, Lilikalā, 5, 65
Kamehameha I, 5–6, 57–59, 60–61, 62–65
Kamehameha II. *See* Liholiho (Kamehameha II)
Kamehameha III. *See* Kauikeaouli (Kamehameha III)
Kamehameha School for Boys and Girls, 90
Kamehameha School for Girls, 90
Kapiʻolani, 99
kapu. *See* taboos
Kapuāiwa, Lota (Kamehameha V), 78
Kauikeaouli (Kamehameha III), 10, 66, 70, 73, 78, 79, 101
Kaumualiʻi, 68
Kawaiahaʻo Seminary, 87, 88–91, *92*
Kekaihaʻakulou, 68
Kekāuluohi, 73
Kekuaokalani, 63–64, 66, 67
Keōpūolani, 6, 60–61, 63, 66, 70, 72, 75
Kīnaʻu, 73
King George's Island, claims of, 20, 22. *See also* Tahiti
Kinney, William, 85
kinship groups, 4–5
Korean Methodist School for Boys and Girls, 90
Kū, 60, 61, 64, 67
kuhina nui, 1, 65, 66, 70, 73–74, 79–80

Ladies Society of London, 46

To order or obtain more information on these or other University of Nebraska Press titles, visit nebraskapress.unl.edu.